SECRETS

OF A

PSYCHIC

No Secrets Held Back

JUNE CAMPOBELLO

DEDICATION

I want to dedicate my book, *Secrets of a Psychic,* to my family who have worked together to get my book published in spite of the setbacks and delays. Granddaughter-in-law Neddy Dommer, was everything during the early days of writing the book; my typist, my grammar police, my editor. Once I had a working copy, Grandson-in-law and Granddaughter, Robert and Stephy Margetts created a website for a blog to provide a place for friends and family to read my work and give me feedback. Then, in July of 2012, Daughter-in-law Emilie Coulter took up the mantel and completed the final typing and edits to get the book in final form with help from Grandson Jerry Barrilleaux. Son Alan Coulter finalized the plans for publishing the final product. Daughter Trisha Dommer also assisted with the typing and editing, but more importantly, her devoted and untiring attention to my well-being, my health, and my happiness made it possible for me to write and to enjoy it all.

To all of you and to my many honored friends mentioned in my book, I send a thank you wherever you are in the universe. I could not have done it without you.

CONTENTS

Prologue

I am seventy-two years old and I am a psychic. Which is worse? I suppose one of these days I must get around to facing the fact that I am getting old. Nothing has brought this to my attention so graphically as the newspaper headline I read yesterday, "Elderly Woman Struck by School Bus." She wasn't just struck, she was killed. And she was the mother of a neighbor and friend. The poor, unfortunate woman was seventy-two. How dare the press call her elderly! I'm seventy-two and you can bet your young arse, I'm not ELDERLY.

So, now in view of that ego-damaging headline, I am reminded again, that 'one of these days' I intend to write about how this all got started and about my unusual experiences as a psychic before my mind goes South and I am that headline. I'm now ready to tell ALL. I've led a life full of wondrous experiences that I have kept tucked away in secret places in my heart and in the journals I've been writing since I was a teenager.

These chapters are not designed to be all-inclusive. To put it simply, there is just too much to tell. I just want to describe a few of the astounding experiences that happen to most true psychics. I want to give an overview of our lives, of the possibilities. These are not out of the norm occurrences for us, we just don't usually talk about them; but I write in the hope that this book will send you on a quest for more knowledge on paranormal phenomena. There are bookstores, your computer and the Internet, and the library for further education.

The stories in these chapters are true. I've wished that part of my stories weren't true, but all of it is documented, at the time it occurred, in my journals. Anything that I was not certain of was left out. I must emphasize here at the start that a few of these stories may seem beyond the bounds of probability. Every detail was gathered by me through personal observation or reported to me by friends that I trusted.

I suppose I am not the little old lady wearing purple and a red hat. I no longer worry about what others may think of me and it is too late to embarrass my mother – she's on the other side. Age has freed me from all sorts of constricting bonds. Names of living persons have mostly been changed. Famous ones who have given me inspiration and guidance I have identified. To have been a tiny partner I in their fantastic lives has been the highlight of my life. What a gift I've been given, to see so many miracles. My contemporaries are rapidly making their transitions. Many have come to me in meditation to encourage me to tell the stories that involved them. Here, now, are my truths. Here are my secrets.

CHAPTER 1

I BECOME A PSYCHIC

I was probably born with my "sixth-sense" well established, but as a child I didn't realize it. I must have had an inborn sense of people. When I recall incidences from my childhood, I know now that I was receiving messages that could only have been coming from that part of me that was psychic, which I later recognized and learned to utilize.

I was ten years old when my father, a dairyman, was badly injured in a car accident on a desolate country road in Arkansas. The other car did not stop. All evening I'd been driving my mother crazy with my crying and screaming,

"Daddy is bleeding!" My mother was indifferent to my pleas, though this was not unusual. She was a stoic, practical Swedish woman, not given to be very sensitive. She constantly chastised me for being too emotional.

When the police came to our door to tell Mother my dad was in the hospital, my aunt comforted me while they drove Mother away to be with him. I worshipped my daddy and was consoled by the fact that help had arrived in which Mother found authority. He and I were always close as he was also fey, like his sister and like me. His sister was my ally.

The definition of *fey*: having supernatural powers or clairvoyance. ("fey." *Oxford Dictionaries*. Online Edition. 2013.)

At about the same time that my father got out of the hospital (they kept them a lot longer back then), I kept asking my aunt why the dark-skinned and poorly dressed people were all crying around me and I was also feeling very sad. My aunt claimed she didn't know, but soon my brother and I were going downtown with Mother and Father to see the other man who was hurt when his truck struck my father's car and drove it into the ditch. She made us get down on the floor boards as we were passing a large billboard beside new buildings being constructed at a crossroad. We could smell the stench and it was really dreadful, but we saw nothing.

Later I heard Mother and Father talking. Then I understood. I was too young to understand, but somehow I did and I told my brother. It was especially horrific! A man was hung there, really only a boy, very young. There was no trial. In those days it was just the white men's story and the black man's story, and who in the sheriff's department believed the real story? Today it would be called a *lynching*, but then again today it would not happen. There is some good in the world, no? But the sad part, and there are many, was the terrible smell that I remember. From that day on my mother and dad drove miles out of the way to avoid that area altogether.

My father's sister lived with our family from the time my parents married until she died, the year I graduated from high school. She read fairytales to us when we were children. She believed in fairies, "the little people," she called them. And she KNEW things. She was sensitive to forces beyond the physical world and I probably inherited my abilities from her. She was born in Copenhagen, Denmark. Her father, a banker, personally knew Hans Christian Anderson and helped finance the publication of his fairy tales. With that kind of a background, she was influential in my psychic development. It is easy for me to understand now why I shut down my psychic development at about the age of ten. There was only discouragement from my mother when I would come out with illogical and preposterous, even comical, predications.

There was the time when my girlfriend developed large lumps on her arms. I didn't say anything to my friend, as I never let my friends know I had these feelings. I was shy, and despite my aunt's encouragement, I kept most things secret, almost as though they were shameful, akin to a wart on my nose. Tell anyone? I think not!

I did tell my Mother I saw big, black "C's" on those lumps. Mother just stared at me. I felt stupid. I'd never heard the word "cancer," but soon my friend was gone from the disease. It was my first introduction to the sorrow of loss. I think of her still.

One does not want to be an embarrassment to one's parents. In the twenties and thirties, psychics were "fortune tellers" and were deemed second-class citizens, and more than that, of the devil. Where we lived in Arkansas the only ones we ever heard of were the gypsies. They often camped in the woods across the street from our house on Avenue D in North Little Rock, Arkansas. At night I watched their campfires and admired their brightly painted wagons.

Most people feared gypsies. Landowners had their acreage littered and fouled, farms had chickens and smoke houses raided. But I was greatly influenced by their moonlight scenes with crinoline and colorful clothes, their passion, their fortune telling, divinations and secret powers. Their customs and beliefs were so different from our Lutheran home life. I never knew of their illiteracy, as their communication was oral in those days. Their women used amulets and talismans, and had occult powers. They were not slow in exploiting this talent by telling fortunes and asking the gullible to "cross their palms with silver." When I started to *read*, I had a difficult time charging for my services because I remembered my mother talking about those "dreadful gypsies, their tea leaves, tarot cards and their thievery."

Mother would threaten my brothers and me that she would sell us to the gypsies if we didn't behave. She told us they used children as slaves. It was no dire warning for me. I'd seen the young ones dancing in the firelight around their elders, and it seemed to me to be the ideal life. What punishment? Get to travel and no schooling? Where was the punishment in that? I was always ready to run away across the street, except I never got up the nerve. Periodically the police came and chased them away. I'd watch the long caravan pull out of the woods and down the hill from our house and I'd cry. My Aunt would tell me not to worry, that they'd be back in a few months and sure enough, here would come those romantic nomads back to our woods. I kept, in my heart, the memory of the dark-haired, dark-skinned wanderers. The first oil painting I ever did was of a gypsy man and woman dancing, with a campfire in the background. So I know I felt a kinship with those people, perhaps from another lifetime.

At the age of nineteen, I went from my disapproving mother into marriage with a man who was uneducated in and combative toward supernatural knowledge. I had a fear of being ridiculed so I mostly kept quiet. I did not allow myself to learn or to accept who and what I was. (I did, however, keep it as a "pastime pleasure" and read continuously on the subject, merely for pleasure.) Time marched on, and in the sixties the messages became stronger and stronger, even clearer.

First impressions were the strongest. On meeting people for the first time I had to be careful not to blurt out, "Your son just stole a lock for his bicycle at the hardware store," or "Your husband sure fancies his secretary." My husband did not like these types of observations when I'd share them with him. Sitting in a church service I would whisper, "Mrs. Smith is pregnant!" He'd whisper back in disgust, "You cut out that shit! You know that's of the devil!" So much for marital support and encouragement. Granted, it might have been unfair of me to marry without confessing to my future husband that I had this dubious affliction, but World War II was the more important topic and the daily life of being a soldier's wife on an army post took up all my time and energy. Besides what did I have? I didn't know.

I first had a son, a beautiful boy, and four years later a beauty of a daughter. The war had ended and we had moved from the army post to Tyler, Texas, birthplace of my husband, now a retired first-sergeant. My days were spent oil painting and tending to children. In those days women did not work outside of the home.

Life in a small southern town, as Tyler was, was very restrictive in the late forties. It was great for raising a family. There were no liquor stores within thirty miles. The streets were tree lined and the city was famous for its roses, azaleas, and flowering dogwood trees. I never knew any psychics, never heard of them. Once in a while a friend would drive to Dallas to consult with one, but I was never invited to go along.

When my son was in first grade, we moved to San Antonio. I developed a whole new set of friends. Several of them went to a palm reader. I sneaked along. I was told that I, too, was psychic – how delicious! The thought had really never entered my mind. My childhood predictions had mostly been forgotten. I thought THAT part of my life had been a part to be ashamed of, that there was something wrong with me. The small daily "knowing" was just a normal thing with me that I believed, perhaps, everyone possessed.

With this professional affirmation I entered a period in my life in which I sought-out other readers, crystal balls, and tarot cards. We moved to Dallas. I began giving credence to my own skills. I did not tell my husband – I felt like an unfaithful wife. I met a well-known astrologer who showed me that in my chart I was born under a clairvoyant sign. Astrology was another new world to me. It's as old as the Mesopotamians, when one could see stars a whole lot better than after the advent of bright lights, tall buildings, and smog.

Then I became acquainted with Suzy, my greatest cohort in "crime." I met her the week after Kennedy was shot in Dallas. She was the first person in my life that I could tell anything and everything. We shared the ability to see into the future and into the past. What a joy it was to have a friend who understood. She loaned and suggested books to help me unravel who I really was. I spent hours at the library. I confided that I was thinking daily of dissolving my twenty-eight years of marriage to a verbally abusive man (by that time he'd become physically abusive). She cautioned me to take it slowly and pointed out that unless he and I could part as friends, I would be condemning myself to a marriage with him again in another life so that we could work out our differences. I believed her. I knew nothing about reincarnation, but of all the hell fire southern sermons I ever heard, the words she spoke frightened me the most.

I rocked – and that's a good analogy – along in my marriage until one night when he broke our shower door with my head. The next morning I decided a future life be damned, and I left home. Thankfully, we were able to mend our fences years later. It took time, of course, but was well worth it. One marriage to him was enough for me!

After thirty years of being a housewife, I was now single and in need of a job. I had no job skills that I was aware of. I was an artist, but that wouldn't immediately put bread on my table. With sheer aplomb I applied for a job at a furniture store, selling them on the idea that with my training in color and design, I could be of service to their customers. I could sell STYLE! The store hired me, and three months later my divorce was final – I was off and running! I'd transformed myself from a timid housewife into a new creature – a SALESPERSON!

Now, being single and gainfully employed, I was free to do anything, even do psychic readings. I would never have been able to read at all when I was married to my husband. He thought those "weirdos" belonged in an institution. My new, metaphysical psychic friend, Suzy, encouraged me. Through her I met other psychics who became friends and also taught me techniques to work with.

My first *reading* was at a wedding shower

given for my engaged daughter. Her friends had called me their second mom and they knew I played around with my psychic abilities. They had seen those books around the house and through the years had asked many questions. I'd told them things from time to time, like where to find a missing item, when they were moving, when they would be hired for a job, or if a certain boy liked them and would call. At the shower they were begging me to tell them something about themselves. So I did. Just on a whim I decided to try the method I'd read about that the famous Edgar Cayce had used. I'd had his course that same year. I'd previously used this for relaxation. It worked! Immediately I "saw" one of the girls sitting beside me on the campus of the University of Texas at Austin; she was almost full-term pregnant. When I said this out loud all the girls giggled. They knew she was pregnant though she was not yet showing. I saw the baby as black and felt weird saying it, but again there was laughter. Her boyfriend, unbeknown to me, was Asian.

My success that evening was heady – I felt at home in this place in my mind and knew that I wanted to use this ability. At first I read for friends, then friends of friends. I was developing methods of understanding and foretelling coming events and past happenings that related to the present. What fun it was!

I bought my first house on my own a year after I began selling furniture. My bedroom doubled as a room for readings, with a bit of drama. Two walls were draped floor to ceiling in red and navy silk and the other two were painted navy. My new furniture was antique red on a white carpet. Brass lamps with black shades sat on the bedside tables and helped with the soft lighting I wanted for ambiance. I placed a tape-recorder on the table to the left. I recorded all readings. I feel that good readers always allow themselves to be taped. We have nothing to hide. Clients also brought their own recorders. I wanted them to have what I'd said with them when they left to listen to later in case they were nervous and might not remember everything. I also kept a candle on the left-hand bedside table and always lit the candle and said a short prayer for protection inviting angels to watch over us for accuracy.

In 1971, two years after I started doing

readings, I had an automobile accident. My car went off the road and into a ditch; the car was a total loss. As I was hurled forward on impact, my head hit the dashboard. I had a concussion that left a deep depression in my forehead that is still visible to this day. My psychic ability took a giant step forward as this blow activated my third eye, a spot we all have in the middle of our foreheads just above the point where our eyebrows meet. The Hindus place their Caste-marks at this spot because it is supposed to be a channel of great hidden power. In my lifetime I have proven to myself that this is a truth.

By the following year, an article was written in the paper describing me as the best psychic in the Dallas area. I'd always been a bit nonchalant about my talent as a clairvoyant. It seemed like a playtime activity. I enjoyed it on my days off and some evenings, and I did not charge for reading – until I met Maya Perez. Maya was a world famous psychic; she is now deceased. She encouraged me to set a price for my time. She said, "A man is worthy of his hire!" She even pointed out that it would increase my credibility as it frees one's clients from any feelings of debt. She was right. I'd received a lot of gifts I did not want. Also, people felt free to call back for another reading, where before they had not wanted to impose. With the money there was one drawback, though – the middle of the night calls from single women in bars wanting to know, "Is this man in the yellow shirt across the bar the one you said I'd meet and marry?" Sometimes it was to tell me that something I'd foretold had just happened. Oh my! It was two in the morning, in the first place, and in the second place, I read from a light trans-state and upon finishing I rarely remember a thing I had said. I did nothing that would alter a person's life, nothing evil.

To this day psychics are barely "out of the closet." In Greek history, "prophecy" meant "speaking before," in modern English it usually implies foretelling the future. Originally, this was "being a spokesman of God," which may or may not have concerned the future. A prophet was the human spokesperson of God. This special relationship with our Maker then led to the association of miracles and supernormal abilities such as seeing into the future. A prophet's main objective was to teach, warn and encourage. Since such telling did foreshadow future events, "prophecy" turned into "prediction." Jesus himself foretold the fall of Jerusalem and the Temple. The Temple fell in 70 A.D.

After forty years of studying and learning to understand the paranormal, I still find the average person reluctant to accept any part of metaphysical occurrences. One fears what one does not understand. For most of my life I was in the closet, hiding my psychic abilities from friends and even my own family. Duke University, long a bastion of psychic studies, has yet to accomplish proven results in any realistic or consistent pattern acceptable to science and to us all. That, in itself, IS the pattern. But I have long accepted what, to me, is undeniable proof that there is more to this world than our practical side will acknowledge.

Opinion polls tell us 85% of Americans believe in miracles and 85% of Americans believe in God. I believe in my God-given miracles. They are truths. This book is written just for the fun of it. I do not attempt to write great spiritual truths, but I do live by them daily, and they are bound to sneak in.

I have had a fascinating life. I have reinvented myself. I was a single woman in my forties just beginning to understand myself as I was becoming obsolete by beauty's standards. I have met many incredible people, many who are still in my life. I have been so blessed!

Chapter 2

Unusual Psychic Readings

I had read many times for a beautiful flight attendant from Washington D.C. She used to fly into Dallas on her days off just to see me, always a compliment and always a pleasure. The regret that I had when I retired was that I might not see her again; but she has honored my decision, does not ask for a reading, and visits me anyway.

At her most unique reading, she was not in my presence, but in her apartment in Washington. I was alone, in Dallas, and meditating when suddenly appeared before me the image of a Victorian woman in a nurse's uniform of the

Crimean War. (I learned this later when I looked up styles of female nurses' uniforms on my computer.)

"And just who are you?" I wondered and asked her out loud.

"Florence Nightingale," she shot back, and before I could ask why she was appearing before me, she continued, "I am living again in this century in the body of your Washington D.C. friend, Lynn."

I asked, as I usually did, if she had a message for Lynn, but she seemed only to want her to know that she had once lived as a nurse in England, and she was proud that Lynn was still carrying on her work of ministering to people's needs when they were on an airplane.

I've often heard Lynn refer to her work as a flight attendant as just being a "nursemaid" to passengers. She does love her work, has been in it for many years, starting back when they were called "stewardesses."

I ended my meditation at that point, too excited to continue. I was eager to call Lynn and relate my startling news. I was not sure how she would react to the information. Would she think I'd gone around the bend? Did she believe in reincarnation? I usually stayed away from dealing with that subject!

I reached Lynn by phone. She is a quick-witted, high-spirited woman and she began yelling, "Oh, my God!" I suggested she go to a library and research Florence Nightengale for any similarities between their lives to lend credence to this wild report of mine. Then she was anxious to hang up, promising to call me back on her return.

Later that day she described her visit to the library as a deja-vu experience. She had sat with a biography of Nightengale before her and she said she felt cold chills running through her body as she compared their lives. It was as if she was reading a story of her life. They were both born in May, just days apart. The photograph of Nightengale showed a small, narrow face with similar features, the same brown hair and eyes – like looking in the mirror for Lynn. Lynn loved Italy and especially the city of Florence. In Nightengale's day, of 1820, girls were not named after a city. It was not appropriate, but her parents were upper class English and privileged so they chose the name they wanted for their daughter in spite of the common practice.

Lynn has flown the world over, many times, in her job as a flight attendant, and Florence was considered a world traveler, unusual for women in her day. Florence lived in Italy, Egypt, Germany, Russia, India, England and in Crimean war-torn Scutari (now Uskudar, Turkey). She never married. Lynn is in her 30s and still single. She told me of their many similarities and believed that she truly received the gift of knowing that she was this famous and ground breaking nurse who changed, forever, the world of medicine by her findings during the war. Florence noted that more patients died from disease than from their war wounds. Sanitary conditions in hospitals were appalling in her day, and she believed it led to disease and fought for change. She'd worked in Crimea for two years. It resulted in Florence's lifelong crusade for nursing reform through formal training, especially in sanitation.

What convinced Lynn beyond a doubt was the eerie feeling of similarity she felt while reading about Nightengale, the ache in the pit of her stomach, the tightness in her throat. She KNEW she was looking at pictures and reading facts of which she was already cognizant.

We would all like to believe that we have led past lifetimes as important people and people who added to the lives of others. It's been amusing to have read for more than one woman who claimed to be Cleopatra reincarnated. I understand the need. Most of us have led countless lives of a common, often dreary, unfulfilled nature. Lynn's discovery was exciting for both of us, to touch on a life so important to our medical world. Florence Nightengale was the first woman to receive the Order of Merit from the British Government. She died in 1910. Lynn was humbled by this information and hopes she can live up to her heritage.

The Opal Ring

I preferred reading in my own home, my own set-up, with a lighted candle. There were times when I read over the phone for a small question, but I never felt it was as accurate as having the person with me. I had many calls about lost objects and I always meditated and called them back with my findings. Many times it resulted in success with locating the lost object. One such call was a little more complicated.

My friend, Naoma, always dreamed of owning an Australian black opal ring. Her husband knew this from the many times she'd admired one in a jeweler's window display. For Mother's Day, he had her pick out one of the large opal gems. The jeweler made a trial design in clay and her husband brought it home for her approval, this first try at a final design. A week passed before the opportunity to return presented itself.

That afternoon the jeweler called indignant, and informed her that she had returned a different stone. The implication was there that she had stolen his opal and replaced it with an inferior gem. She was devastated. The stone he had chosen had incredible fire and was the fulfillment of her lifelong dream. This was really puzzling. She had not noticed any change as the ring had been in a box in a drawer. She had picked up the box and had not looked closely at it again. She was certain no one had touched it, not even her husband who had been out of town on a business trip. She called me with no specific question, just in tears over the situation. I offered to meditate on it.

I called her back with information. I'd been unable to pick up exactly what had happened but knew for certain that both she and her husband and the jeweler were all honest. I'd found that her angels were protecting her from that particular stone because it held bad vibrations, but that she must wait only two weeks and all would be resolved.

I so admire Naoma. She is a tall, beautiful girl of Cherokee extraction. When she was in her late teens she had been a performer at the Aquarena Springs in San Marcos, Texas. She wore large jewelry with flair. Today we would call her a bling-bling female.

Just one day before the two weeks were up that I'd predicted, the jeweler called her with an apology. He'd just returned from the National Gem and Mineral Show in Santa Fe, New Mexico. While talking with a fellow designer there, he'd told him the story of the bad-looking opal his customer had returned to him. His friend was quick to point out that it had been a mistake on the jeweler's part. The clay had leached out the moisture in the stone, leaving it lifeless. He advised placing the stone in glycerin until life returned to the stone. My friend was delighted, but told the jeweler that she wanted to choose a different stone since learning that it had bad vibrations for her. He was thankful for her choice because when he had taken it out of the glycerin to examine it he accidentally dropped it and the stone had shattered on the floor. She found an even lovelier stone and a ring was successfully made for her.

Once again angels were successful in delivering us from evil. And what if I, in the beginning, had told her the stone was evil. Would she have believed me?

A Very Large Man!

It was in the club at the Marriott Hotel across from the Dallas Furniture Market in July that I met a very unusual man. A couple of fellow salesmen were with me. We'd been viewing all the new lines of furniture and were parched and tired, and went into the bar to have a drink. This strange man was sitting at the bar. He watched us for a time. I was conscious of being stared at, but was surprised when he came over to our table and introduced himself. He said he was from Boston and claimed to be in business with Jeane Dixon's husband. She was a famous astrologer and reader, now deceased. He asked me to book him a reading for the next day.

I asked him, "And you are a friend of whom?"

"I don't know anyone you know," he said. "I'm in town on business."

"But this is impossible," I answered, "I'm not wearing a sign on my butt that says, Fortune Teller?"

"I've been watching you. I always recognize psychics. They have very different eyes."

"Why don't you get a reading from Jeanne Dixon?" I inquired.

He laughed, but did not answer. The man was very heavyset with dark hair and eyes. He resembled a Lebanese fellow I'd known, but was a bit more ominous looking. I did not feel the need to explain why I could not read for him the next day – Sunday – but I did tell him that I was having a pool party and would be busy with guests.

My daughter and I were always dreaming up excuses for a party and this one we called a "Wet-Tee-Shirt Splash Party" – in other words, no bras, ladies. Our friends played along with us just to see what outrageous party we would come up with next.

He said he would pay me double. I'd heard that before! That didn't faze me, but when he said he'd bring his swim trunks and a tee-shirt that got through to my weird sense of humor. Three hundred pounds, or thereabouts, in a bathing suit struck me as hilarious. Would my pool water rise over the top with all the weight he had distributed on his suffering skeleton? Would his large drawers fall down to his knees if he tried to suck in his tummy for the ladies?

"Okay," I agreed, "Come ahead, but it will have to be a short reading as I will be very busy."

He actually came! He had his swim trunks on and a loud, yellow tee-shirt. He joined us in the pool. He brought smiles to everyone's faces and was our party clown.

I read for him later that day. He had mostly business questions. He said I was fabulous and better than Dixon (aw, shucks!). He was pleased, but where was my double fee? I called a cab for him. He did not pay me. Was I supposed to ask for my money? I had never had that problem before. I never let it happen again. At that point I stopped being shy about asking, up front, for what was rightly due me. The first time that I asked, I imagine I felt what I it must be like for a prostitute collecting her first fee. It was very personal, but quickly I became adjusted to the routine. I did learn to enjoy having my clients "cross my palm with silver."

The most unusual reading I personally ever had for myself was with Maya Perez in 1972. She was visiting Dallas from California where she had started her career as a tea-leaf reader in a tearoom. She was an incredible woman. She was exasperating at times – pushy, talkative – but a tiny, pretty creature from the island of Barbados. I never learned her lineage, but she was probably a mixture of Spanish and African extraction. It never really concerned me. Who cared?

I had read about Maya Perez in the daily paper. She was having an evening seminar and giving personal readings during the day. I chose to have just a reading as I could not afford to do both. I was single and working at my first job after my divorce.

I went to her hotel for my reading, excited to meet her and see how she worked. She greeted me with hugs, as if I was her long-lost friend. (I later learned that she did this with everyone she read for or met.) Immediately she said we'd lived a lifetime together in Egypt as hand maidens to Cleopatra. (At least we weren't Cleopatra!) She said we would be journeying to Egypt together – seven months later we did!

I was elated to hear her say that I was also a psychic. To be admitted to her world was the ultimate statement of her reading that day. I was being knighted by a Queen! She told me that one day I would write a book (and here I go). She said that my son was also a writer. (Only two years later he wrote his first book, a textbook for special education teachers.) She said that my daughter, too, was an author – still to materialize. She swatted me in the stomach, alarming to my shy (at the time) nature, and said I needed to lose the tummy as it gave away my power. Now, years later, I'm embarrassed to report I am still giving away my power. Whatever the hell that means!

She seemed aware that I had chosen a reading instead of the seminar so she invited me to dine with her as her guest and attend, free, the evening session.

Maya remained my close friend for the rest of her life. She was always a generous friend. For years afterwards she stayed at my house and did her readings when she was in Dallas. She rewarded me with many gifts, bought groceries and paid restaurant tabs over my protestations. She gave me, and all our guests, foot rubs and hugs. I received lots of encouragement with my first venture into working as a psychic. I found the extra money very helpful. In turn, my charging for readings made me conscious of wanting to do my best so I wouldn't feel like I shortchanged anyone. I became a vegetarian as one is better in tune with the universe when one is free of animal flesh. Maya Perez added to my life. Bless you on your way, dear soul.

My Client, the Marijuana User

I learned a valuable lesson about the improper use of recreational drugs when I read for a young man in his early twenties who came to me with many problems. I immediately sensed that he needed more help than I could provide. He needed "big-time" advice. In my circle of metaphysical friends was an Australian psychic healer. He did a great deal of counseling with drug abusers. I was concerned when my young client confessed that he did a lot of pot (he was a gorgeous stripper for Chippendales and also was the son of a dear friend of mine) I stopped the reading with instructions for him to go to the Australian's home for help. Looking back and thinking in practical terms, why did I not call the man to get his permission to send this troubled person to him? How could I have presumed that he would be at home and be receptive? I seemed to have just been following orders from beyond.

The door of the Australian's house had been opened with, "Come in, I've been expecting you." My friend's son thought I had called to announce him – I hadn't! He rang me at work the next morning to report that he was never going to smoke again. My friend's son had found, and believed, that he had been possessed by a vicious, unprincipled spirit, because he had not been in control of himself. He now knew what had influenced him to commit the terrible acts he had come to me to discuss the day before. He was elated and relieved. He felt that he had been released from his problems.

The healer stopped by later that same day to tell me more details about the exorcism he had performed to drive out the entity. He added that he had warned any more smoking and losing control would invite the spirit to return with dire results being the consequence.

Several years, three wives and four children later, the young man killed himself with a handgun, leaving behind a mother, father, sister and brother who have never recovered, and perhaps many more loved ones and fatherless little children. They all reported that he had been back into drugs. What a waste!

How I Got My Geode

And now an unbelievable, but true reading. I hardly know where to begin, but I know I must not leave anything out of this event that I consider the most implausible of my entire life.

My career as a psychic reader and my life as a furniture salesman were kept closely guarded from one another. I never told a customer at the store about my strange talent so it was surprising to me when I found myself telling a young woman who was selecting a whole apartment of furniture. Telling her was not appropriate. But, I did it anyway.

She was a diminutive blonde, blue-eyed lady of about thirty years old from some state west of Texas. I'd never met her before. It was her first day in Dallas, and she knew no one in the city. That morning she had rented an unfurnished apartment in preparation for attending her first year of nursing school. She hadn't picked me as her salesperson, it had just been my turn on the floor. I felt very fortunate because she was purchasing so many pieces, never imagining, albeit unaware, she would change my life for the better. (Was she an angel unaware?)

We chatted as she chose pretty pieces for her apartment, even lamps and accessories. I told her I did readings (where did that come from?) and she, I must choose the word, DEMANDED to come to my home that very night for her own reading. The store closed at nine and I had worked all day, but I couldn't refuse her when she'd made such a large purchase and was still in the store finishing up with the credit office. She followed me home in her car.

So we went to my house. I invited her in and after my usual preparations, including putting a fresh tape in my recorder, we began. I said my prayer and counted myself down to my alpha level, and before I could speak, this deep, masculine voice came out of the mouth of this little lady. My small, soft-spoken feminine client was speaking, at least her voice box was being used by someone or something, most certainly a man's voice. I listened in awe.

It was a message for me! It said to take the "rock" from my bookcase in this room, a geode from Mexico that my mother had given me, and go to an address the voice then gave me and to go NOW. Then silence.

I sat up, startled, turned off the tape and set it to rewind. I shook the lady awake. She was slumped over on the bed. We listened to the message together, she heard it for the first time as she had no memory of being used as a medium. I opened the bookcase and took out the Mexican geode, not a very unusual or a very beautiful rock, just an average crystal center surrounded by black rock.

We were both excited even though it was after ten o'clock at night. I told her I was going to that address and asked if she wanted to go along. She said, "Just TRY and leave me behind!"

So off we went, not having a clue of what to expect. The address was across town, but in a neighborhood I was familiar with, having lived there when I was married.

After ten-thirty we found the address, expecting to find the house in darkness. Through other houses were apparently asleep, this one was lit up inside and out, with a porch light shining outside. We rang the doorbell. We did not know what we could possibly say that would not make fools of us both. We were giggling like school girls in our nervousness.

A smiling, dark-haired lady opened the door and invited us to come in. She said she had been expecting us! We didn't say anything. What could we say? We only had questions. She introduced us to a tall, smiling man and two ladies. They made us feel welcome.

The living room was dominated by a large canvas pyramid perhaps eight feet across. I'd seen them before on television, in homes where hippies lived. These people did not look like hippies. I knew that pyramids were a popular place to meditate. The belief is that pyramids hold powerful healing energies.

Inside this one sat a woman in the yoga position. She gestured for me to join her. I was actually very frightened, but I knelt down and crawled into a spot in front of her. She did not speak, but held out a hand that I just knew was for my geode. The one part of this most bizarre evening that still haunts me, years later, was that her eyes were an electric blue, and when I made eye contact with her they were flashing a bright, blue light like the lights on a police car. I was mesmerized. We sat in silence while her eyes continued to flash. I do not know how much time went by. For me time stood still. I was weak-kneed when I came out of the pyramid and stood up. She handed me back my rock. She stood up also and invited me into the kitchen. My furniture client was having a bowl of soup the woman had been cooking in a large pot on the range. I believe it was lentil soup. It was delicious. Here was also some wonderful homemade wheat bread.

I asked the woman from inside the pyramid what my geode was good for. She seemed startled. "You don't realize, do you?" she said, "It is so powerful it can do most anything."

We learned that this group of people was followers of the Siddha of India, Baba Muktananda. She told us that the voice we heard on the tape was his. My companion freaked out! I was spellbound. Baba was from the lineage of the Siddha beings that are perfectly fey. For two decades he had been considered one of the great saints of India. He has now made his transition. I felt greatly honored that somehow he knew or heard my prayers for wisdom and granted me the great gift of this special energy my geode was capable of putting out. After that night I began to read with greater clarity and effectiveness.

What dimensions were we in this night? All five of these people had new names given them by Baba. They were all vegetarians. They complimented me on being one. How did they know? I did not tell them. I listened to them in tremendous awe. They were not trying to have us join them nor were they looking for donations. Their sole purpose was following Baba Muktananda's request to serve me, a request they'd received in meditation inside the pyramid.

We left after midnight. We were both hyper. Understandably, I lay awake for hours after my client left. In my own meditation I asked what to do with the geode. It felt hot in my hands. I received the instruction to use it in my readings by placing it on my abdomen, which I have done ever since. At first, I felt a bit foolish. Seldom did anyone inquire about it though, and it has become normal for me. Years later, I read with sadness that Baba Muktananda had died and I wished him a safe journey to the other side where I know he was welcomed with joy.

I never heard from that furniture customer again. I suppose she was too freaked out by the experience. I expect that her only purpose in my life was as a means to get the message through to me that night – the message to take the rock to the pyramid. It needed to be activated. I didn't call her either. What could I say? I figured the ball was in her court. I think she dug a hole and dropped that ball into it. Or was she an angel? Perhaps.

Chapter 3

Ghosts and Spirits

When I was in my forties, selling furniture for Haverty's Furniture Co., living alone and doing readings in the evenings, I happened upon a reading of ghosts. "Ghost" comes from the Old English, "Gast or Soul." Of course, there are ghosts – ghosts of good and bad intentions. Ghost lore encompasses a wide range, as the forms and habits of ghosts are incredibly varied. In ancient times, ghosts were linked to crop failure, disease, bad weather, and even death. Today many people think of them as souls of the dead, draped in the sheets and rattling chains, moaning and howling; and they feel any appearance is basically hostile and a dangerous occurrence. This caricature had grown from the gothic fairy tales that frightened us as children, and from Hollywood horror movies. Surprisingly, that caricature remains current in spite of new investigations and millions of sighting from reliable witnesses.

Parapsychologists (psychic people) see ghosts and spirits on a regular basis. I do. We think of them as messengers and we attempt to interpret what they might be trying to tell us by their appearance in our material world. In my favorite Shakespearean tale, Hamlet's deceased father appears to him, trying to make him aware of his murderous stepfather's involvement in his death and to accuse even Hamlet's mother of condoning the same. Of course, this being fiction, Shakespeare had him speaking plainly. However, it is not easy for them to appear; it takes a great deal of energy. And for them to actually speak, in an audible voice, is extremely rare.

Our questions about ghostly appearances remain mostly unanswered. Perhaps someday we will learn for certain, exactly what happens after physical death and we will be able to finally welcome any contact with the spirit of a loved one that had made their transition.

A Haunted House

Frank Mendle, the same manager at my workplace who asked for my help with his wife's breast cancer diagnosis that I described in another chapter, once again called me into his office and closed the door.

Sheepishly, he asked, "Uh, do you know anything about ghosts?"

"What's going on?" I answered.

He told me that he believed they had a ghost in their home. I was very interested. He had a ten-year-old son and two smaller daughters. They had heard what sounded like the closing of a heavy door – theirs was not – then the sound of heavy bolts being slid across that door. Now it was happening every night just after they were settling down in bed. For a time they'd become accustomed to this nightly ritual and had decided that they had a friendly ghost. Now, new things had begun.

One evening at the dinner table an invisible force levitated their silverware, moving it across to the other side of the table, then dropping a piece of silver into one of their glasses, splashing out some of the contents. The children's milk would tip over, soaking a plate of food. His was tired of it. The children were amused, taking it all in stride, laughing at these antics. Mrs. Mendel was not laughing. The family dog, as well, was quite upset, howling miserably. Frank found it difficult to eat with the howling going on. He found it increasingly uncomfortable to be in his own home. His favorite painting was always on the floor with its nail still in the wall. Other pictures were tilted sideways. I immediately thought of poltergeists, but that is an invisible force that usually occurs in a home where there is a teenager. Their children were ten and under.

What Frank told me next sent cold chills down my spine. Not a good sign. He said that just that morning he and his wife discovered a large, reddish-brown hand print on the ceiling of the children's room, and beside it a dark, red mark encircling three parallel lines. He though it looked like dried blood. He moved the children's chest of drawers to the middle of the room, under the marks, to check if their son could possibly have made the prints with his finger paints even though the hand print was larger than Frank's own hand. No way. The ceiling was much higher than the boy could have reached.

I become very concerned. It was obvious to me that whatever supernatural force was producing this phenomenon was desperate to get their attention. Now it was frightening all of them. His son talked about seeing a large dog that would disappear when he tried to pet it. Their dog was turning into a quivering wreck. This was going too far. And why were there bloody-looking prints in the children's room and not in the master bedroom? Was it a warning?

We read that ghosts can't kill us. Yes, they can! They can frighten us into having accidents! If they have the strength to move heavy pieces of furniture, as this one had done, then they could cause a large piece, like an entertainment center, to fall on us. They can cause us to flee in terror and perhaps fall and injure ourselves. This appeared to be a genuine and strong ghost.

Frank, the husband, was an accountant (C.P.A.), a very serious breed of people. I know because I married one in 1982. They are not inclined to play practical jokes. I believed him. Frank probably wet his pants when he saw those ominous bloody-looking prints, though I didn't ask him.

I told Frank of several methods to rid a house of an unwelcomed entity – garlic, bleach in small cups in all four corners of a room, talking to the unwanted when he felt its presence, and commanding it to leave the premises. Frank tried them all, feeling foolish talking into, what seemed to be empty air, the children questioning him, his wife in tears.

When he spoke with me again a few days later, he wanted to know if he should consider moving. They had been contemplating a move, anyway, to a larger place where each child could have a room of their own. I agreed it might be time.

I might never have heard more about it as they'd moved a month later, but after three months of having their old house on the market with no offers, their real-estate agent reported that she was having trouble getting anyone to look at it. Prospects would walk into the living room, do a wheelie and go right back out the door. She said the house felt cold and smelled bad. She's tried deodorizers. She'd tried candles, but they wouldn't stay lit. She'd tried having the carpets cleaned. Nothing helped bring in prospective buyers any further than the front room. It had been standing vacant for ninety days. I offered to go there and see if I could help – I'd been curious anyway and interested in seeing the house.

I talked with Cedric, a parapsychologist friend, and his friend, a principal of a Dallas public school. They had done an exorcism or two and they agreed to visit the house with me. After all, what did the owner have to lose?

The next night the three of us, not knowing what to expect, drove to Irving, Texas, where this troubled house was located. We took flashlights, a tape recorder, a card table, three folding chairs, a camera and a Ouija Board. We had a notebook and several pens. We were PREPARED, like good scouts – we thought!

Upon opening the front door we were instantly assailed with the coldest, foulest air I'd ever experienced. It was a warm summer evening outside, but it was freezing, a certain sign that an otherworldly presence was in this house. We first checked the children's room. The dark red marks were still on the ceiling. The handprint appeared to be that of a very large person, a man we supposed due to the size of it. I took photos, as the others set up our card table in the children's room, feeling that this was the hub of the activity. We placed the Ouija Board and started the tape recorder. Cedric and I each put a hand on the planchette. The principal held the notebook and a pen ready to write if the board could make contact with the spirit.

A Ouija Board consists of a rectangular board with letters, numbers and punctuation marks printed around its surface. It uses a free moving planchette or indicator, ours being a plastic affair about four inches in diameter. Usually two people place their second and third fingers lightly on the edges of this piece. It can be worked by one person as it is then guided by one's subconscious or perhaps a supernatural force. The planchette moves around the board, stopping above a string of characters until it spells out a message.

Please be aware I take these boards very seriously. In no way are they toys. DO NOT play with them. The messages only come from one's subconscious, but our minds can become very inventive and even evil.

So we began. Immediately the planchette started moving in circles, wide ones at the beginning, then tightening up and slowing down. We asked to speak to the spirit in the house. We sat in silence. After about two minutes, finally, haltingly, it spelled "Deb Faver." We had a name!

We thought this was a female. More quickly it moved to the "No" printed on the board. We spent about an hour asking questions, getting nothing but the planchette moving in circles. Eventually we thought to ask him if he could read or write. We got a quick "No."

I said, "Let me try to talk with him by going to my Alpha Level."

So far we'd had tough luck. The camera, when focused on the ceiling, would not flash. We'd forgotten the microphone for the tape recorder. This type of bad luck seemed closer to normal than not, as I've read many accounts of the same things happening to other investigators.

Nevertheless, when I relaxed in my folding chair I immediately went into a trance. My friends sat in their chairs and relaxed into a meditative state to help me by providing their energy. After about ten minutes they shook me awake as I was crying and sobbing. I had a lot to tell them.

I'd been down in a waterwell here under this very room. I was experiencing what had happened to Deb those many years ago. This was a farm then, long before this land was developed into neighborhoods, streets and houses. The well was walled with rocks that were wet and slime-covered. I knew instinctively that Deb had fallen in. He'd been doing some repairs and had lost his balance. I felt myself fall and hit the water far below, just as he had done. It was very dark except for a small circle of blue sky far above me. I tried to inch my way up to the daylight overhead. I braced myself with my buttocks on one side and my hands and feet on the other side, but the rocks were mucky, repulsive. I would crab-walk up a few feet, lose my handhold on the rocks and fall back into the water. Then, out of the cold, I would brace myself once more. I'd recover my breath and start toward the light, lose my grip on the rocks and fall again. Soon my hands were bloody.

My dog (Deb's dog), a bloodhound, was crying up overhead, beside the well. I lived alone with my dog. He was an old dog, but desperate to help me. I could see his beloved face peering down at me. We'd been on a rabbit and squirrel hunt earlier in the day, and we were both tired. He was faithful. He sensed I was in mortal trouble.

I was experiencing how it had been for this man and his last thoughts were transferred to my brain. His weight was a detriment. He was a large and sturdy man and his heavy work boots added extra weight. I could not get them off in the narrow space. My bloody hands told me that my more tender feet would soon be bloody also. I had built this well in a former life, and I knew the rocks had sharp edges under their slimy surface. Once more a steep climb, almost to the top that last time, but I fell, my strength all gone. I came back up out of the dark water only once more, and then was gone.

Today, twenty-five years later, I can still feel those gruesome rocks surrounding me, my watery grave, my terror and helplessness. I still mourn for the faithful dog that starved to death by the well, waiting for his master.

My friends held me until I stopped crying and I was back to full consciousness. When I could compose myself we once more used the Ouija board. Now we knew to ask only yes and no questions. We asked if the land had been his farm. "Yes." We asked if he lived alone. "Yes." Did his dog get hungry and leave? "No." Did the dog starve to death? "Yes." We wanted to know if Deb had meant to harm the people who had lived in this house that had been built over his well. "No." Was he guarding them by closing that heavy door each night? "Yes." Did he just want to be part of a family? "Yes." Did he love them? A quick, "Yes." The children saw a dog, was this his? "Yes." We asked him how old he was and the planchette showed us six and then two, sixty-two. When we asked him what year it was, he showed us 1794. We asked him if he could manifest his existence other than on the board. "Yes." We asked him to shut and bar the door like he'd done for the Mendles.

We sat in the silence and perhaps fear. Nothing happened. Suddenly, our Coleman lantern sputtered and went out. Nothing! We turned on flashlights and asked Deb, via the board, if he was tired, after all we'd been working with him for over an hour. Getting an affirmative answer, we blessed him and told him to leave this place and go to a higher plane. We pointed out that he was dead and belonged with the people from his lifetime. We said he should look around to find the shining light and walk into it.

Poor tortured soul. Like most hauntings, he meant no harm to the occupants. He was only trying to communicate his presence. He seemed to love the Mendles and locked their door for them at night. He put a sign on the children's ceiling that said, in effect, "These three, I give my hand on, I'll see after them as they sleep." We decided to do an exorcism, for his own good, to free him to go on, instead of being earth bound.

Webster's Dictionary: exorcism — the expulsion of supposed evil spirits from persons or places by certain adjurations and ceremonies. The word exorcism came into popular usage with the famous pea-soup movie, "The Exorcist." Seeing that movie we learned, to the surprise of most people, that the Catholic Church had always recognized possession and ghosts and had regularly been at work eradicating this evil. There were times when my children were small and had real terrors, that I was sure I should call a priest, even though I was Lutheran.

Deb was gone! He was no longer answering us. I did not sleep well that night. I found myself grieving. My two friends reported a sleepless night and both confessed they had cried when they were alone. One happy person was my boss. His house sold ten days later. His wife had cried though, over Deb's tragic story. She wished he would come back and live in their new house to protect them. (She's a sweet and tender lady who writes Western novels.)

They went back to the house once more. They told the spirit of Deb to come and get in the car and go home with them. They told him he could live with them in peace and thought Deb was in the car as they drove away because their dog was whimpering on the floor. But they heard nothing to indicate his presence in their home. My friends and I think he had gone into the light. I hope so. Did he get lost on the ride to the new house with them? Does he wander the world alone, isolated from the land he loved? I don't think so, but I'll never know. Good luck, Deb, wherever you are.

A Ghost in a Motel

In 1982, I married Sam, my soul mate. We were driving to Washington State where we would fly from Seattle to Alaska, on our honeymoon, leaving our car in Seattle for a couple of weeks. Our second day out from Dallas, we had carelessly driven until dark without a hotel reservation. Honeymoon bliss? When we began stopping for a room we found all the motels along the highway were booked up. We were over an hour's drive from the next city at that point. We felt as Mary and Joseph must have felt. At least I wasn't pregnant. The final motel offered us a room in a no longer used building across a courtyard from their new facility. The new rooms were fully booked. The old section, though closed, still had an old bed and some old furniture in one guest room. They offered to make up the bed for us. It was either this room or drive still further and we were very tired. With clean sheets on the bed it seemed that we should be comfortable enough for one night. It was a very LONG NIGHT – the place was haunted!

Psychics, like me, are more sensitive than the average person. Soon I was beside myself, literally! I was pacing. My husband offered to check out and drive on. It was definitely not a honeymoon suite. Outside, the weather was a lovely August night in Washington State. In our room it was icy cold. Luckily, since we were on our way to Alaska we had sweaters and coats in the car.

Sam brought in warmer clothing. We turned on every light. At first I was fascinated. I walked the room, tuning into the strange vibes, becoming more sensitive. There were noises just below one's normal hearing level, sobs and what sounded like crying. If my new beloved husband hadn't believed in the supernatural before tonight, this certainly made a believer out of his nervous butt. He also heard the low noises.

We were so tired. We decided that if we went to bed and snuggled up together we would fall asleep. I went to the bathroom for my tooth brushing and flossing. I came screaming out of there and into his arms. In the bathroom I saw a very faint, but ominous large, dark shape like a bear walking upright on his hind legs.

When I calmed down Sam investigated the bath and found deep claw marks in the woodwork around the door and running all the way from the lintel, over the door, to the floor. It looked as if SOMETHING had been imprisoned in the bathroom and had tried, repeatedly, to free itself – to tear its way out.

My husband was presently in the process of installing, in the home he was personally building for us, rough pecan wood that he had planed into boards. He was baffled about what could possibly make scratches that deep in this hard, oak trim. He's six foot tall. He could have made them, but only with a sharp, heavy tool!

We talked of German Shepherds, Dobermans, and Great Danes. They could have reached that high, but their front paws would have not had the strength, with standing upright, to have clawed that deep. We talked of bears and shivered. I thought of the large, dark shape I'd seen. We were in BEAR COUNTRY. This bear seemed to still be here in spirit, still suffering, still trying to free itself. The air in the bathroom was foul. Ice would not have melted. This spirit felt harmful and dangerous. I took snapshots of the claw marks, which I have kept to this day.

I tried to take some comfort that this was an animal that had likely died here and not a human. We were, after all, on our honeymoon. Perhaps a good romp in the sheets would dispel the doom and gloom hanging about. Of course, nothing happened between us. It's a mood killer to think a ghost-bear might, any minute, leap out of a bathroom and into one's bed.

Finally, we fell asleep. I woke up a lot. So did Sam. We should have just made that hour drive. We even talked about it again, in the wee hours. Where had my psychic powers been hiding when we stopped here? I should have had a hunch. I, of the tiny bladder, managed my first all-night marathon as a no-show in that horrible bathroom.

At first light, the hour known to me as "sh't" a.m., we left. I hoped that I had helped. In the night I'd talked with that poor bear's consciousness. I hadn't actually seen a bear, just a vaporous shape. It could have been a very large man left in that bathroom to die of starvation. I surrounded it with light and told it to go in peace.

Chapter 4

Healings and Such

Most of us could be healers if we would only try and believed we could. Talents are given to all of us and different ones to each of us. I know that if someone has the desire to be a healer it indicates an innate talent for healing, especially those people who have warm hands – energy in their fingertips. Many have the natural gift of healing and merely need to acquire the skills that come with practice. I think God gave most people the talent of healing and few of us really make good use of it.

Yes, healing challenges the laws of nature, but Jesus and multitudes of our forefathers demonstrated that it can be done. Augustine said,

"A miracle is an action going beyond the ordinary laws of nature."

An Illness – or a Ghost??

I discovered my gift while taking Jose Silva's *Mind Control* course in 1972. I told my fellow salesmen at the furniture store about a success I'd had in class. We were given the name of a person who had an illness and were asked to name that illness and then do what we, mentally, felt should be done to take away that illness. I was given the name of a woman and her location, city only, and told by our instructor to mentally examine the body and find the problem area. I was successful in determining that she had a mass in her right lung that I felt was a tumor. The instructor told me to take care of it. We'd been taught several methods of removing unwanted obstructions in humans and animals. I used an easy solution – I just mentally reached into her lung and took out the tumor, threw it in a trash bag and sewed her chest back together. This was all done mentally, of course, as the woman was in Chicago, Illinois. It was an awesome and humbling experience, but I felt good about it and a week later it was reported to us that the woman was cancer-free! I'd achieved the goal – and it was heady!

Bragging about it was a mistake. I was not mentally ready to do any work in that field. But word got around, and a couple of days later one of my bosses called me into his office and shut the door. Uh oh! He told me that his wife was scheduled to have a breast removed because of a diagnosis of cancer, and he was hoping for a divine intervention. I was deeply distressed that I had no choice but to offer to TRY and help. I stressed that my success had probably been a fluke. When I say "MY" I do give credit to God, our source, working through me. I didn't confess to my boss that I feared my unskilled "try" might cause her condition to worsen – what a foolish concern, as that cannot happen. I believe God helps the innocent because SOMETHING led me to the right path for her.

That night, at home alone, I got comfortable, counted myself down to the Alpha Level as I'd been taught in class, said a prayer, and then mentally asked to have the woman's breast in my hand. I, again, mentally removed the cancerous tumor. I imagined myself holding a hammer, busting the tumor to dust and scattering it into the heavens. Then the thought occurred to me to pick her up and put her on a cloud and leave her there. I thanked God and counted myself back down out of the clouds, back to my conscious level. I was so relieved – I felt successful!

By morning, though, I was afraid to face her husband. What could I say to him about what I'd done? Not to worry – he called me, right away, into his office and closed the door. "What did you do?" he said, "My wife is on cloud nine! She's calling her doctor. She cannot feel the lump and claims she's healed!"

Her doctor could not feel a lump either and an x-ray confirmed that there was no tumor. The surgery was cancelled. The weirdest thing was my bosses' statement, "She's on cloud nine," – because that's where I'd left her!

You would have expected I'd have become a healer, since I'd been so successful in that area. But, instead of success giving me confidence, it had the opposite effect. I had experienced myself as energy and I felt I had left my body! I was terrified! I didn't have the courage to heal. It was a long time before I tried another healing, even for my family. Looking back now, I believe that my God-self must have been very disappointed in me. I wanted to have spiritual integrity, but I also wanted to be liked and not have people afraid of me. Humans are uptight about parapsychology, and especially healings. One fear is that a person who has these abilities can also read minds. Rubbish! Also, there's the fear that psychics can tell such things as if one has on dirty underwear. Not for me – that possible rejection. Not for me, that's like Shirley MacLaine going out on limb. I'd rather be in the safer zone of being a reader. Healings are so much more involved. All individuals have their own timetables. Some of us actually enjoy our poor health, having created is as if it were a child. Others are working through a karmic situation. Many of us don't want any changes from what we've learned to live with, as it seems better than the unknown. Still when a serious need arises in my family, I am there with help for them.

I've done hundreds of small things for my extended family: headaches, sprains, faster healing of broken bones, once even athlete's foot. But I have been careful to swear my family to secrecy. They have gladly kept my secret, as they too did not want to be laughed at for something so far left of the norm. I have been their "closet" healer. For them to believe in me has always been enough.

The very latest thing I've done is put pink light and then blue light into the tiny lungs of a preemie baby boy in trouble with underdeveloped lungs. I did this from my home. I did not need to go to the neo-natal ward in the hospital. He stood at the edge of death, so close to going over that the doctors ordered the mother to make plans for it. And now he is at home (this life) with his mother and twin sister. This was due in large part, also, to the many devoted people who were praying for him. It all works together for healing.

Healing My Own Eye

I've been blessed with several miraculous healings for myself. The most miraculous of all was in 1985. I was living in the Texas Hill Country south of Austin with my new fabulous husband. I developed temporal arteritis, a condition that affects the eyes. An artery in the temple becomes inflamed and can cause blindness. Over a couple of days I experienced a gradual curtain-lowering effect in my left eye. I'd never had headaches so I should have known something was happening when I had severe pain in my left temple. Only when the sight in my left eye went completely black did I call my doctor. He immediately sent me to an ophthalmologist. She did a biopsy and confirmed that my problem was temporal arteritis. She said that we were too late to save my left eye, the nerves were dead. She put me on massive doses of Prednisone to help save the right eye. She said it usually follows that sight is lost in the other eye.

Nothing from my life experiences up to this point should have given me the belief that I could do anything about total blindness – that sounded so final – but even in my deep shock I refused to believe that perhaps, in a couple of days I could go from 20/20 to complete darkness. I asked my husband not to tell anyone I had lost vision in my left eye, the first step in attempting a healing! We did tell my son and daughter, but no one else. We were concerned about any negative thoughts – thoughts are powerful energies – that might be sent my way concerning "dead nerves." I also did not want pity to throw me into depression. That same day I also called the headquarters of the Unity Church to put me on their prayer list. I called several metaphysical friends: one a member of Edgar Cayce's organization, the Association for Research and Enlightenment; an exceptionally gifted group of healers in Argyle, Texas; a chiropractor friend in Richardson, Texas who was blind himself; and a healer in Arizona – all my "Big Guns."

Not all at once, and not immediately, but little by little, over a period of six weeks, I began to see. There were tiny flashes of light at first, then dim shapes and finally clear, beautiful, wondrous SIGHT. Never again will I take my eyes for granted. My ophthalmologist was incredulous. She looked, over and over, at my left eye. She still saw the nerves as dead, but with my right eye covered I could read an eye chart, even better than before. It's been fifteen years and still she calls me her "miracle girl." She asked me once if I would come with her to a class she was teaching at a medical school. She never mentioned it again. Can we suppose she could not obtain permission? The medical world recognizes healings, but my case was a little bit over the top.

When I was first blind, and just opening my eyes in the morning took calm out of my new day, I received the encouragement I sorely needed. I was visited by a vision of a very handsome American Indian from a century ago. It happened when my husband and a woman friend of ours were climbing Enchanted Rock, a granite outcropping near Fredericksburg, Texas.

I felt the need to sit down and rest and asked them to walk and climb on ahead, and I would catch up with them later. This was a strange thing for me to do. I soon found out why. We'd come to a peaceful grove of trees among large boulders at the base of the largest granite outcropping. I sat down on a large, flat rock and before I could even shut my eyes I saw before me in a soft mist, a large, half-naked Indian. (Later I saw the movie "The Indian in the Cupboard." I was startled by the resemblance – not the same face, but the same clothing.) I was aware that this was an apparition. He was very handsome except for an obviously missing left eye. He told me, not with audible words, but in my head, that he was on his way to Oklahoma with his spouse and child because game in this place was becoming scarce. How could I know he was from a century ago? It was instantaneous. I just KNEW he was a messenger from that era of our country. He spoke as though what had happened back in the 1800s was happening to him now. He said they would be joining their tribe in Oklahoma. He told me he'd been blinded by an arrow in a battle, here at the rock, and he knew how I felt. He said I would regain the use of my eye. At that moment I KNEW that I would.

I'd had my moments of doubt, of course, as I couldn't picture the "how" of it. In the midst of the challenge of my blindness I had forgotten my training. We need only to see the perfect results. It's not for us to reason the HOW, leave that to spirit. My Indian friend got me back on the track, picturing the end result as I now remembered I should. Alas, I never even spoke to him or thanked him 'till I saw him fading from view.

I think, perhaps, my friend herself a strong psychic, who walked while I rested, had lent her strength to this helpful manifestation. She might not have even been consciously aware that her energy was being used for the Indian to appear to me, though her higher self would have been willing. It takes an inordinate amount for souls to become visible and usually this vision comes and quickly goes because of this energy drain. What a reassuring gift he'd given me: a certainly of healing. Looking back, I muse, could he have been me in another life? Or maybe a relative? I had a male friend with whom I'd often talked about a life we believed we lived together as Indians in the Southwest. He, in this present life, was my hairdresser for eighteen years. Could it have been him? More about my eye later.

The Arizona Healer

Another healing for me personally. My friend, Suzy, told me there was a great healer coming from Arizona. I called for an appointment. I just wanted the experience of seeing how they worked. This was several years before the healing of my eye. My five-year-old grandson was with me when I drove to Ft. Worth on my day off for an afternoon appointment.

The healer came in; he seemed like a very kindly man, although very formal. He asked questions. He passed both hands about six inches above my body and announced I had a tumor on my uterus. I did! I had not mentioned it to the lady who made my appointment. I had an appointment with my gynecologist for the following week to discuss removing it. What a strange talent this wonderful man had. He never touched me, just those hands passing up and down my body. I was so in awe. I know now that with a good healer, one does not necessarily need to be a believer. I was a skeptic in those days as it was early in my serious development as a psychic. I'd lived twenty-eight years with a husband who scoffed at all things out of the norm. So I was learning to be open to new experiences.

Then the healer told me I was just starting into my change of life. I was! I'd just had a couple of those dreadful things called "hot flashes." He said, "I will take you through your change of life rather quickly today." That phase has remained current in my mind though the years. It's been over twenty years and I've never had another hot flash. With a few more passes over my body, he said he was finished and left the room. His assistant told me to lie still for about ten minutes, as I would be dizzy. I didn't feel that I was. After five minutes or so I became nervous over my grandson being an imposition and I sat up. Sure enough, the room spun. I lay back down for a time. Soon I was able to leave. I gave the assistant my donation. The healer did not charge, however, it was expected that one give a donation. Mrs. Perez, a psychic, had taught me that a man is worthy of his hire, and I wished I could have given him a great deal more. When I called him years later for help with my eyes, I did send a nice fat check.

I will never forget my drive back to Dallas. I felt as though I was drunk. I should not have been driving, especially with my precious cargo, my grandson. My daughter would have been alarmed, but I delivered him safely home and went to my home and to bed. Suzy called and was overjoyed at my tale of the day's events. "You received a healing!" she exclaimed, "It always makes one dizzy if there's been a healing."

My gynecologist examined me again the next week and found no tumor. He decided his first diagnosis must have been wrong. At that period in my life, the early seventies, I did not have the guts to tell him I'd been to a healer. Shame on me. And the wonderful development – I've never had another hot flash, mood swing, or any other symptom of change of life problems.

Because of my good experience, when I heard there were two Filipino healers in town, I took a girlfriend along to see if they could remove a tumor from her right breast. The healers allowed me to watch. I'd seen a T.V. special accusing these healers of being fakes. They were shown to perform a lot of theatrics including knives, cloths that could hide chicken entrails, blood and more blood. They spoke no English. I saw them, these healers in front of me, pull something from my friend's breast, very bloody. I did not examine it, of course, but my fingers remained crossed.

The bottom line on these mysterious men in my friends case was that later in the week she called me. She'd been back to the doctor. She confessed to him – good girl! (Made me ashamed of my shy butt.) Her doctor commented he'd seen stranger things happen. He did not laugh at her. Her tumor was gone and has never come back.

As far as the Filipino healers on T.V., they were made fun of and perhaps they encouraged it. They might have been amateurs looking for a cheap ride on the Hollywood train. Who knows? I sure don't.

Cat Tales

An interesting footnote to my temporary blindness was the reaction of my cat, Amy. We'd named her Amaretta de Sarona, which quickly became the less-of-a-mouthful, 'Amy.' An important cat deserves an important name! She was a longhaired apricot stray that showed up at our door; a male, wee kitten. I had just lost my cat of many years and here came Amy. For sixteen years she was my familiar. Webster' Dictionary: familiar – a close companion. We had always thought Amy was a female!

Of course, I'm a lot like a cat myself. I too, am independent. I don't always come when I'm called. I bathe a lot. I love to lie on the sofa and watch the birds outside my window. I eat when I darn well please, and at bedtime I love to snuggle up to a tomcat for the night. Of all my cats, in all my life, Amy was the most psychic. She was my healer.

She was quickly trained as a kitten to sit by the door and cry when she wanted out. Only when she was very old, with arthritis, did she require a sandbox. Even in the rain she would go out, always, stopping by the door on her return for me to towel dry her. She loved water. When I would water the flower beds she would jump in front of the hose. She followed me all day, around the house, around the yard, unless I was vacuuming. Then it was under-the-bed time.

My then new husband had never had a cat. He was a bird watcher and objected to accepting her into our household. She seemed to understand she could be on borrowed time if she hunted, so she never caught a bird. She watched them from the front windows, dreaming of chasing one, swishing her tail, but she never put her dreams into action.

Our counter in the kitchen was curved; the narrow end, perhaps four feet in length, was her favorite domain. She watched me cook and waited for treats, like water off a can of tuna. Company who disliked cats would scream at me, "The cat's on the counter!" I assured them that area was her place and she'd go no further. They kept a wary eye on her. She disappointed them. She ate on her part of the counter and drank water there. Of course, they never got invited back, except for relatives – ugh. When she was old and feeble, her last year, she could not jump up and she had a few falls before discovering she could climb up in my husband's recliner – whether he was settled there or not – and leap across a foot of empty air to her food bowl. I learned not to wax the counter as she had a few slides and crashes to the floor. Finally, she ate on the floor in her familiar bowls.

I'm actually allergic to cats. She instinctively knew that. She never got up in my face. As a young cat she slept on a bedroom chair, later at my feet on the bed. I was seldom ill, but when I was, she would not leave my side.

All the time that I was blind in my left eye, she walked around with her left eye closed. Everyone was amazed. Friends came by just to confirm what they'd heard about her. They'd even examine her eye to see if perhaps she had an infection. When I regained the use of my eye, she no longer kept hers closed.

T.V. nights were her favorite, then it was nap-time. After she died, oh, that was the blackest of days! She still laid in my lap in the evenings, though out of the body. Most always I'd had visits from my cats when they were on the other side. But Amy was the strongest of those little souls. I could actually feel the warmth of her when she was alive. It's been several years and I do not notice her often, except when I'm not feeling well which is seldom. She's still protective when it is the most important. She still cares. She still comes to me to help heal me.

God wants us to be free of every painful illness. Perfect health is natural. Disease is simply DIS-EASE. We are not at ease when we are ill. God wants us to be whole. To be a healer is in the highest realm of human compassion. If your interest lies with this service, read all you can on the subject. Our libraries have whole sections on healing. Then, as the age-old advice goes – practice, practice, practice. There are laws against healing without a medical license. I believe you help who and where you can, and do your healing in private. Keep it in private. And God bless you. Our own physicians are dedicated souls, but they cannot be everywhere every time and they can use our help. God will not let us make a mistake.

Chapter Five

Witchcraft
The Good, the Bad, and the Ugly

Please have nothing to do with witchcraft! My apologies to all the good and caring witches of the world, but I am convinced this type of magic is not for the amateur or the irresponsible. It is difficult to separate the good from the evil. There is too much temptation to drift into the dark side. What is evil anyway but a matter of definition? Good or evil, I want nothing to do with witchcraft. Are they both a reality? Yes, and I definitely know that they both exist. I have had several contacts with both sides and have always come away with an unpleasant feeling. First, a good witch tale!

The Good

Back when I sold furniture as my primary source of income, I worked with a young man, John, who became one of my best of friends. He and I exchanged metaphysical books and during lulls in the store we discussed them endlessly. There were many authors that we loved, but our favorite was Dennis Wheatley. We read every book available by the British author. Stephen King scared us delightfully with *The Shining*, and to this day I still enjoy such a read.

John was not clairvoyant, but still very aware. We both were interested in witchcraft for a time in the early seventies. During those earlier years, I did enjoy a few minor successes with "spells and charms." These being small incantations as in "please call me," or "I want a date for a party Saturday night," and "make my hair behave." I did nothing that would alter a person's life; nothing evil. I actually, at one point, even considered joining with a large group of practicing 'Wicca' – witches – in the city, but my strong Lutheran background and my family precluded that endeavor, and I gradually drifted away into concentrating on my psychic work. I later discovered it would not have been my scene. (I had a few frightening encounters, told elsewhere in this book, and decided I wanted no part of witchery and the dark side.) Perhaps my higher self (God) intervened. John, however, always showed a strong interest in the black side and called himself a "black warlock," a male witch. (In truth, a male is also just called a witch.) He seemed drawn to the evil, needing a whiff of sulfur to give his soul a thrill.

Soon he and I began to date, surreptitiously. Management frowned upon pairing up between salespersons. It was delicious fun to greet one another in the morning at the store, as if a night had passed since we'd seen one another, secrecy being a childish thrill for us.

I had to spend three days in the hospital – today it would have been an outpatient thing. Each of my hospital days I expected him to visit. Where was he? Visiting me was an unspoken must. He sent flowers. The third day there was a box of candy from him delivered by another saleswoman. She reported – as we females stick together – that he seemed busy talking on the phone to a woman and that he was leaving early each day for cocktails at a bar she'd heard him mention. It was "our place." Hell hath no fury!

Once out of the hospital, I put my best "ice queen face" on and went back to work! I never wanted to date him again. I was cold enough to freeze the mercury in a thermometer and I vowed revenge. My bad inner child, that I usually kept imprisoned in my mental labyrinth, was loose and creeping out of the castle's keep. I enlisted the aid of my best friend Lou, who had similar interests in the occult. Together we conspired to make John impotent. What high school girlish fun! I found some of his hairs left between my sheets from before I went to the hospital – no proper spell is complete without such intimate accruements. In this, our first and only attempt at Evil witchcraft, we did a bang-up job, "bang" being an appropriate word for that area of the anatomy.

Several days later, our victim, with whom I'd resumed a guarded communication at work, was conversing with our manager. I joined them. John touched a place on my neck and said, "I've come in the night to drink your blood," in his most Dracula-like imitation. I shot back with, "And you don't know what I've done to you!" He turned white and pulled me back to the privacy of the lunchroom, a favorite place for a chat, if unoccupied. "Please, please," he moaned, "I've never had a problem before. Please undo what you did. Now I know it was you who caused me this trouble. Please!"

I did promise to undo it. But, here was my proof he'd been fooling around. I never dated him again, and never was tempted to try my Wicca powers. It was enough to know that I could. I should have turned him into a bullfrog when I had the chance.

The Bad

On one of our many visits to Oklahoma City, my male friend Dee and I met with a couple of witches who owned a metaphysical book store. They had been friends of Dee's since high school, but they hadn't been in contact with one another in many years. They had reconnected recently and when he mentioned he had a psychic friend, they insisted he bring me for a visit. They called several times demanding that we drive up, but Dee declined. Finally, he felt that he could no longer put them off and we set a date for dinner. Dee and I discussed how strange it was that we hadn't readily accepted the first few invitations. Something had held us back, though we didn't realize they practiced Wicca. We really knew nothing about Wicca. Little did we dream!

We pulled up, in Oklahoma City, in front of a small, nondescript two-story dwelling. It was a very hot August evening, but winter crept into my blood when I walked through their door. Why didn't I just leave then? It felt cold and unwelcoming, though they seemed nice enough. Something nudged at my consciousness when a small child drifted briefly into the room. I was struck by an overwhelming feeling of sadness when they introduced her as their daughter. I judged her to be about four. She was a silent child with a white, calm face and eyes that seemed vacant. I tried to talk with her, but they excused her explaining that it was her bedtime. It wasn't a school night. Why couldn't she stay up longer? Before dinner? Strange! I decided I did not like these people. Why didn't I call Social Services the next day to report my concern? I wonder now, but then I felt like it was none of my business.

I was distracted at dinner. I think we ate spaghetti. That part of the evening is hazy. From what I do recall, the dinner conversation was directed at me – they wanted details about my psychic work. Dee wanted to reminisce about his high school years with our host. The friend kept silent like the little girl. More questions were directed to me. I was being *interviewed* and I was uncomfortable to say the least.

When they asked if we were ready to go see their store, I was ready to change the scene, but wondered about the little girl upstairs. They said she was asleep, as if that would excuse the fact that she was being left alone. Then the four of us drove to the shop leaving that small girl at home, ALONE! Did the woman even ever go upstairs to see about her? I didn't remember her doing that. I asked if she was coming along with us. The said, "No!" as if shocked that I asked. It seemed that she had never gone with them.

It was a nice shop with the usual types of metaphysical books and paraphernalia; pewter wizard statues, wands and crystals, decks of tarot cards and a great assortment of candles. I purchased a black candle in the shape of a devil for my friend John. I had forgiven the hospital adventure.

Then they opened a door at the rear of the shop. It led down a broad flight of stairs to a basement. Comparing notes later, both Dee and I had the same recollection of the stairs being twice the normal width, wider than his outstretched arm span if walking down the middle. If I had outstretched my arms, I could not have touched a wall on either side. It was my practice to look for and hold onto a railing; there were no railings. The walls on both sides and the ceiling were plastered with six inch stalactites with protruding spikes, poking out from the walls and down from the ceiling. It was an obvious attempt to create a cave-like mood as one descended to the basement.

When we reached the basement, my left hand was bleeding. There was a gash in my palm. The woman remarked that she had seen me grab at the sidewall on the stairs and cut my palm on the stalactite projections. I knew better! I did, later, most certainly remember walking down the center of the wide staircase. I was most proud of my unconscious, I thought, making all those stairs without support. She produced a box of tissues and solicitously, it felt, took from me several blood-soaked tissues. Such a lot of blood from such a small cut, less than an inch.

When my hand was taken care of, and I looked at our surroundings, I was aghast at the room we had entered. The floor was painted black and in the center, painted in luminous white, was an upside-down pentagram! My blood turned to ice. A pentagram does not, outright, mean evil. It is a star with five points that usually symbolizes power. Having one of the pentagram's points projecting upward symbolizes man's body with arms and legs outstretched and the dominance of our divine self. This pentagram was reversed and upside-down; having two points projecting upwards which is a symbol of evil that attracts malevolent forces for help in doing heinous spells. The two upper points symbolize the horns of the devil.

This basement was pure horror to me. I looked around in disbelief. An altar draped in black velvet held a skull, a large dagger and a jeweled goblet. I could not tell if the skull was animal or human. I'd never seen this as part of reality; I'd only read about it and seen it in low-budget movies. I felt like laughing and saying, "You've got to be kidding!" But this was no joke – I was too cold. I knew I was seeing the actual articles, and I wanted to run screaming up those stairs. I have never been more frightened for my personal safety and for that of my friend, Dee. He seemed only amazed, but his face was ashen with alarm, as though he thought he should be alarmed. I knew all this was distressing to him because he saw that it was alarming to me. Why did these people want us to see this place? Did they think I would love it?

They were obviously proud of this room and wanted me to give them my blessing. How could I? They probably believed I had supernatural powers, which I could use to bless their work up to a stronger level. There are so many misconceptions about how we psychics work.

What shocked and distressed me the most (and Dee too, upon later conversation) were the DOZENS of upside down wooden crosses and one giant metal cross suspended upside down over the altar. My Christian upbringing recoiled!

We didn't stay long. It was damp and cold and I was nauseous. We used me as an excuse from anymore looking around and made a rapid departure, saying that I was ill. There was no conversation in their car on the way back to our car that was parked at their home. If you've ever ridden for miles in silence with a mate who was in a snit and no one was speaking, you will understand how awkward the atmosphere was inside that automobile. It was obvious that they were furious with us for not fulfilling some anticipated reaction that they had built up in their minds about their secret basement room.

They let us out of their car in silence. Their house was in darkness; no porch light to welcome them home, no light on upstairs in the child's room. We did not hug each other as I am accustomed to do after dinner at a friend's house. Again, strange!

Through the centuries psychics have automatically been thought of as witches. There is no correlation between the modern psychic and a witch. I did not know what they had in their minds. I can only surmise that they wanted more from me than the blood that they collected on the stairs. I couldn't speak and I could see that Dee, at least pretending, was in shock. This was his best friend all through high school turned into a stranger. When I think of witchcraft, to this day, I think of the dark side because of these people. Dee saw how it could change his best friend into a different, distant, unknown person. He now wanted nothing to do with witchcraft. If all this seems strange in the telling, then think how strange it was in actuality. I don't remember even thanking them for dinner. I do know we never heard from them again.

The minute that we got in my car we were all talk. We both talked at the same time. At first we burst into nervous laughter, hysterical laughter really, and we wished for a drink. Dee was apologetic since this had been his friend and his idea. I would have none of that; it was a shared decision to visit. I should have picked up on it. We alternated between laughter and deep psychoanalysis of their character, however unqualified we were. When we reached our hotel, we had what I call a *stiffner* (drink) and then to bed when the discussion drifted into ridiculousness.

The next day my hand was completely healed. We couldn't even find a scratch in my palm! We talked about how much it had bled. Dee realized how he'd bragged to them before-hand about my being written up as number one in my field in the Dallas paper. He pointed out that they probably believed the blood of a powerful clairvoyant would be most powerful to use in casting a spell. I could not believe that I might have useful blood, but we worried about possible repercussions – but better safe than sorry!   I meditated and put protection around my blood in Oklahoma and myself and I put on a heavy cross necklace and did not once take it off until several weeks later. I also sprinkled salt in each corner of every room in my house, a powerful protection against evil.

In Anne Rice's book *Merrick,* she writes about the power of blood. Even though *Merrick* is a work of fiction, Ms. Rice thoroughly researches the subjects in her writings. She has studied, as I have, extensively and bases her fiction on facts. Starting on page 269, the main character says, "She fixed you, man, made you fall in love with her through witchcraft. Damn, I should have never let her keep that bloodstained dress. No wonder she wouldn't let me touch it. It had your blood on it. Oh, what a fool I was not to see what she was doing. We even talked of such charms together. Oh, she is beyond all patience. I let her keep that bloodstained silk dress, and she's used it to make an age-old charm." Rice, A. (2000/2001). *Merrick.* Ballantine Books. pp. 269-270.

Several years later, Dee and I remarked about the fact that neither of us had ever heard from that strange couple again. I've wondered about that dear, sad child who was alone that night. What were those people? Black witches for sure. What did they do with my blood? Good, I can hope – but what about all those upside down crosses?

The Ugly

I once read for a very socially prominent woman in Dallas; I won't even mention her husband's area of work as I do respect my clients' privacy. She was around thirty and very beautiful. She was seeking advice on leaving her husband and hoped I could be of help. She was becoming increasingly frightened of him. She confided that he was heavily involved in black witchcraft and hoped I would believe her. With my experience in Oklahoma City I had empathy. I had not been aware of the many covens in Dallas, and did not learn of them until later. After my experience with Dee's friends, I became alert to any mention of witchcraft and at one point I'd become friends with a man, another artist, who was a member of a coven, but at that time it still seemed a bit hokey to me, even with my own experience. Then, too, I'd done a lot of reading on the subject. After Oklahoma and this pretty lady's story I lost my innocence about it all and became active in pointing out the difference between "white", a loving coven, and "black", a satanic cult with unearthly powers.

I first listened to her, the pretty lady, with reservations, but my higher conscience soon had me taking her seriously. She said her husband had a private office in their seven thousand square foot home. No one was allowed entrance, not even to clean, not even her. He took care of it himself. Once she'd caught a glimpse of a star-shaped drawing on the floor as she watched him enter his room. I thought, "Oh, a pentagram." She asked me if I thought she was "around the bend?" I'd started picking up on her vibrations and I knew she was telling the truth.

She related that her husband would come home in a foul mood, and furious at someone he'd had a confrontation with during the day. He'd have terrible temper fits, screaming the man's name and lock himself in his private room, usually overnight. A day later she often read in the paper that that man her husband had been screaming about had had a heart attack or a massive stroke and had died. She'd dared tell no one until now as she told me. She wanted to leave him, but was terrified of him and frightened for her two small children. I felt immense sadness. I did not see her leaving him. I suggested she should get away from him, but saw no safe avenue and cautioned her to take it slowly. I felt helpless; calling the police would only cause her peril.

The next day her husband called me. He wanted a reading. Had she confessed to visiting me? Had she been followed? I wondered about it and felt frightened. I'd not advised her to leave him. Spirit had stressed to me to have her take things in a slow motion untill she could feel safe about leaving. I told him I did not read for men. Not exactly true. I did live alone and did read lying down on a bed, so I was cautious about clients. He did not take no for his answer, saying he could not believe I didn't read for men and called again and again. He offered to double my fee, and then tripled the offer. I'll admit I was curious; Spirit did not say no. So I gave him an appointment. My daughter came to do guard duty, staying in another room.

When he arrived I could have picked him out of a crowd and not needed any psychic abilities. He was in a black tux, on his way to some formal occasion. He was blue-eyed with jet-black hair (dyed?), a slight bump on his nose – but attractive, and a tight-lipped unfriendly mouth; but the whole effect was distinguished and all together handsome. He had that confident aura of a Donald Trump with a large dash of malevolence. I hated to think he was anyone's mate, let alone a father of two children – this smug, self-absorbed, artificially tanned, distinguished man.

I lit more than one candle for this session. Of all my clients he was truly the most evil. He was over the top, as though he was an actor playing a part of someone obviously pretending to be evil. He would have come across as a 'fake' had I not seen his photograph numerous times in the daily paper. When I saw Tom Cruise in *Eyes Wide Shut* years later, I was transported back to that night. This man could have played that part to perfection.

Spirit kept an icy finger on my tongue. He pumped me for info on his wife's reading. He learned nothing. I answered business questions. He asked about other men in his field. Information seemed blocked about certain men, perhaps because I truly believed he was a killer for real. A lot came to me about his childhood that he agreed with, but all in all it was an unremarkable reading, perhaps colored for me by his wife's revelations.

I did not receive much information that I considered valuable, such as definite dates and helpful insights into coming events. Clairvoyants want to believe all readings come from a higher source, but realistically and practically, we are bound by multiple factors – our health on that day, the weather and even preconceived notions. All of these factors can enter into a reading because we are human. He seemed pleased, however, and paid me triple as he'd promised and tipped me generously as well. When he was out the door I did my Pontius Pilate routine – I thoroughly washed my hands with soap, for I had shaken his hand, plus been in his presence. Water is purifying.

I never saw either of those people again for I mentally pushed them away. I'd often see pictures of the two of them at society functions dressed formally, smiling; they looked happy. Her eyes were sad though, and I guessed she never found the courage to escape. I always surrounded her with light and with love and prayed that she and the children were safe.

Yes, there are evil witches operating everywhere today. They are not just the stuff of B-rated movies. They are REAL. They can do severe and deadly damage. They use their powers to manifest in a very real and negative fashion. Should we have a worldwide witch-hunt? Of course not! I have simply advised myself to just stay clear of them.

Chapter 6

More Ghosts

I've seen spirits many times in my own home. One gets used to them when one is a psychic, but when I saw my deceased father very plainly in my bedroom one night, I was actually frightened. He had been dead for fifteen years! I asked him what he was doing appearing to me. How cold I was! He'd always been a happy, laughing man. He then laughed and told me he was going to fly with me from Dallas to California; and then he just faded away.

I was planning to attend the wedding of my nephew, my dad's grandson. I almost cancelled my trip. I thought he was going along in spirit because the plane was going to crash, and he would then be there to help me go to the other side when I was killed. Not a comforting thought when about to take a plane ride. I searched for reassurances. When I remembered that he was smiling I took that as a good sign and went ahead to the wedding. That was one long, nerve-wracking plane ride, but of course nothing terrible happened and the wedding was beautiful. My father, though now welcomed, has never appeared to me again. More the pity, I loved him.

My Deceased Aunt's Visit

One time when I was meditating my precious aunt came to me in a vision. She was my father's sister who had lived with us since before I was born until she died in 1940. I was not frightened. I was enthralled. I loved her still. She said she'd come to take me, spiritually, to see where she lived on the other side.

She took my hand – I felt like Peter Pan as we rose up into the air. I remember looking down from the ceiling and seeing my body sitting in my recliner. I knew I was having one of those *out-of-body experiences,* and I was spellbound!

There is a theory that we all leave our bodies nightly, in deep sleep. We are just not consciously aware of it. It's called OBE, an out-of-the-body-experience. To explain it is impossible in terms of our present physical world-view. It is certainly an altered state of consciousness. In sleep we slip effortlessly in and out of our bodies, safely anchored by a silver cord. Most do not remember the adventure when we awaken, but some have the blessing of recalling the experience. After the first time it happened to me with recollection upon waking, I no longer feared death. I knew at that point that I will survive when I leave my body for the last time. What a gift.

My aunt took me to the other side. I wish I had the proper words to adequately describe that realm. The colors! Oh, the colors! I'm an artist, and there's nothing in our world to compare with the colors I saw – an endless kingdom of wonder. I planned, while there, to remember those hues and try to mix them in my studio. But, of course, I could not. They are not earthly colors. I asked Jan Price, author of *The Other Side of Death,* and she agreed the colors are indescribable. Her book about being on the other side is a wonderful read and could dispel any doubts you might have about what happens after death. It belongs in everyone's library.

With my aunt as guide, I visited buildings constructed of a glass-like substance, with one wall fading seamlessly into another. Walls crossed over each other and were transparent. It was awesome to my artist's mind, a palace for the spirit. I wished my nephew, the architect, was with me. I could have wandered and wondered there for hours, but we moved on to gardens of magnificent flowers and fruits. I felt more reverence there than when I visited the Sistine Chapel in Rome. I had nothing to compare with this place. Bellingrath Gardens in

Alabama comes to mind, but even that garden cannot begin to touch it.

She told me that she was alive again, on my earthly plane, in St. Louis, Missouri. How could she have willingly left this heaven? She explained that this was the natural order of things and she'd chosen to come back. In her life with me she'd always walked with a cane, and at times with two canes, from crippling arthritis. This was in the days before hip replacements. In her new life she was no longer crippled. In my life with her, she had long hair, down to her waist and red. She was also redheaded in her new life.

I wondered how this could be, her here with me in Heaven and yet alive again on earth. She explained that the spirit that was here with me now was but a fragment of her total soul, a part of the soul that always remains in the heavenly realms. I believe that explains the feeling we mortals all have, this longing for "Home." A part of us always dwells there.

When I asked her for her present earthly name and where exactly she was living in St. Louis, I got only a sad smile. No answer. Oh, how I would love to go there and find her, but I realize that cannot be. How would one feel if a stranger came to our door claiming to be a relative from a former life? We'd freak out and call 911 for a strait-jacket!

Souls on the other side do not want to frighten us by suddenly appearing in our bedroom, our sanctuary, as my father had done. He expected me to understand, but it would frighten most of us. I wish he would come back. I've promised not to panic again, but it hasn't happened. He might have been given that time only. So, our departed family and friends come to us mainly in dreams. If the dreams are strong enough to wake us, then their importance must be addressed. It is difficult to always understand what they are trying to relate to us so they will return again and again until we get the message.

The Furry Ball Presence

My daughter has the ability to see ghosts as well. When I lived and worked in Dallas, my daughter had a key to my house. She often told me that, once more, she'd seen "my" ghost (the ghost that she thought lived in my house). He was this small, basketball sized, round, furry ball that would go scooting across my front room and disappear under the sofa. Her husband would laugh at us and call us kooks. Years later, he exclaimed, "I saw it! I saw it!" She didn't need to ask what. She just hugged him and rejoiced that she, at last, had confirmation that *my* wee ghost had moved to her house. (This confirmed for me that ghosts come in all sizes.)

This unusually shaped ghost seemed to be in whatever home my daughter was in when it wanted to manifest. We've never figured out what it was and what it meant. It might be just a ball of energy that's shy. (Here I go, getting flaky.) At her first house after she married, she would often surprise an elderly, dignified man in a top hat and long, black overcoat that would then dash around a corner and disappear as she was coming into the house.

She has a lot of contact with the other side and gets messages of love from a close relative that died of AIDS. She doesn't agree that she's psychic, but I know that she must be. This friend with AIDS, who knew he was dying, told her that whenever she saw a Schneider van it would be a sign that his spirit was with her. The Schneider trucks are few in this place in Texas. It's not a Southern company. They had shared a favorite song, and often, when she sees one of these vans she's also hearing their song on her car radio at the same moment. She gets weepy and rejoices that he is safely across and happy.

The Visit from the Brothers

In the fall of 1987, my husband and I were enjoying a weekend with friends who lived in an old restored farmhouse on a ranch near Brenham, Texas. It was a beautiful place with huge Spanish oak trees, lots of green pasture grass and a pair of large tanks – the Southern name for ponds – where black and white Angus cattle drank. It was a bucolic country scene. Who would ever suppose that not one, but two angry ghosts were lurking in this idyllic farmhouse ready to attack a guest?

We had spent part of the day in Fayetteville for their fall festival, "Lick-Skillet Day." The parade was a child-like joy with lots of cowboys on well-groomed horses, homespun beauty queens in organdy dresses and over a dozen of old Ford Edsels, the car design that failed. I couldn't imagine there were any Edsels left outside of a museum, and these were polished to a gleaming shine. Like Lake Woebegone, Fayetteville, Texas and pie for twenty-five cents a slice – heaven! The men folk fished the tanks in the late afternoon and at twilight we had a real Texas barbecue on the lawn, complete with beer for all.

Around ten thirty we all settled down for a long, fall night's slumber. My husband went immediately to sleep, but I was only pleasantly tired. While I laid in the darkness reviewing the day, I became aware of two men in the room – I knew they were spirits. They wore overalls, though, and not shrouds. They felt hostile, antagonistic, as if looking for a fight. At first, I was only curious. But as one grabbed me by an arm and tried to drag me out of the bed, I became afraid. Strength in a ghost? The second man grabbed my other arm. They shoved me back and forth, laughing in a maniacal glee. I was terrified. These were no friendly disembodied spirits, but more like demons. I wasn't thinking that they were out to kill me, but nevertheless I shoved at one of them. His face was icy-cold – and I lost it. I started shouting, "You're dead! You're dead!" They continued to laugh, but not mirthfully, just wretchedly. My screaming woke my husband and a couple of the other guests, who came running into our room. The phantoms in overalls disappeared. I clung to my husband, cold and shaking. He explained to the other guests that I'd had a nightmare and everybody went back to their rooms. I did not go to sleep easily that night!

In the kitchen the next morning I poured myself a cup of coffee and carefully questioned my hostess. Had she ever seen or heard anything unusual in this house? She was not aware of my screaming in the night, but she smiled nervously at my query and even asked me, "Have you seen a ghost?" I fibbed to her and said I had not. I was not willing to talk about my shocking experience. I felt like my hair was still standing on end. I knew I was probably pale so I left the kitchen. Unlike my favorite martini, I was stirred AND shaken. She was not the type to discuss such things, but I KNEW she'd had SOMETHING happen. She'd been given the chance to ask me more and hadn't.

That afternoon we went for a drive with our hosts. At the edge of their property they pointed out a very old frame house set back from the road. It was unlivable, but had never been fixed up or torn down. They told us that this house used to stand where their house was built at the end of the 1800's. It was too old then to be added onto or made livable so it was moved into the pasture. Our host went on to say that they bought the ranch after the previous owners, a pair of old bachelors, had died.

I felt a chill. Here was my explanation for the two ghosts in the night. If I'm ever invited back for the weekend again, I'll have pity for them. I will try to contact them and help them cross over to the other side. Obviously they've become earthbound. Was it a coincidence my attention was called to that old house that had been moved and that mention had been made of the brothers? I think not.

The Mission Church

I'm not sure that this next tale involves ghosts, more like a malevolent spirit.

I flew to San Francisco with my favorite gay friend, Dee. He was, at this time, a salesman for an oil company, having left the furniture sales floor where I worked. When we traveled together we always booked one room, just as good friends. In the mornings he would do my hair. (I was sworn to secrecy about that talent. He'd been a hairdresser in his twenties.) What a joy for me to look professionally styled. He was a bossy friend and insisted on choosing my clothes. He also ordered for me in his favorite restaurants in the Castro District, the gay area of the city.

When I finally remarried in 1982, leaving the furniture business and Dallas, leaving Dee was one of the drawbacks. I was losing not only that daily contact, but there would be no more trips to Oklahoma and elsewhere. No more late nights together watching the *tele* or just giggling like a couple of school-kids. He had always scoped out the men for me in a bar, in those my single years. How was he able to tell me which men had great equipment? How can one tell sizes? Is it really feet? I was not often able to test out his theories as he was also an aid to chastity – he never let me out of his sight, professing jealousy.

At the airport in San Francisco we rented a car and drove to Muir Woods – beautiful, like a temple under those tremendous trees. The next day we drove south on Route 101 to Highway 1 for ninety minutes into downtown Carmel. What a haven for lovers. I wished I'd come here with one. It's glorious scenery. I loved the art galleries and the good restaurants we found. The shops were eclectic in this seaside hamlet.

We wanted to visit the famous mission-style church. On this, a Monday morning, it was empty of tourists. When we walked in the huge front doors we were instantly struck with a blast of cold air, not like the mild ocean breezes one felt outside. We looked at each other in surprise, both thinking the same thought... "Something wicked this way comes" – and it ain't earthly. We stopped.

There was a PRESENCE and it definitely was not friendly.

From a side door on our right a black robed priest burst in. "Get out of here!" he yelled at us.

"Are you closed today?" we inquired.

"No! But you get out of here!" Then, "People like you are not welcome in God's house!"

Yes, we got out of there in a rush. Dee thought it was because he was gay. Priests are often psychic. Paranoid!

I thought it was because I was psychic and it was something he picked up about me. He might have believed I was *of the devil*. Paranoid!

I believe it was a psychic emanation from the very walls of this aged mission. What horrors had taken place there to leave behind that coldness? It may go back to when the Spaniards were in charge. If I ever meet Clint Eastwood, their former mayor, I have a few questions for him.

John

My former boyfriend, John, the one I'd put the impotent spell on, died by his own hand. He shot himself. We had shared metaphysical books and discussed all phases of that philosophy so many times. He'd often promised me that he would visit me after he died to prove to me that he still existed.

He was a Baton Death March survivor of World War II. He'd spent four years in a Japanese prison camp in Manchuria. The Japanese worked these prisoners in a factory and he'd learned to speak their language. He was crippled from that experience and wore a metal leg brace following several attempts to repair a knee that his captors had permanently damaged. They had repeatedly beaten him on the same leg, a habit of ritual torture they practiced. When finally freed at the close of the war and back home, he had several reconstructive surgeries and two difficult knee replacements. The doctors told him they had no further choice but to remove his leg, above the knee, he opted for leaving the earth by way of his 357 magnum.

He had tried to kill himself several months earlier, but was unsuccessful. It was two in the morning when I got the call from him that he'd failed to kill himself, but was bleeding a lot. We no longer dated, but we remained friends. He called, drunk, saying that he'd aimed for his heart, but the heavy gun had misfired into his leg, the same one as his knee problem. (Is that bad luck or what?) I woke my daughter to help me, went by and picked her up. Together, we found him in a pool of blood. We managed to get him up and drag him down the stairs of his second floor apartment. I drove his bloody body to the hospital. Looking back, now, I wonder why we didn't just call an ambulance! This was before the days of EMS. We could have used help, but he was a close family friend I suppose we thought we ought to get him there. People react strangely in emergencies. Also, we even said, in our sleep-deprived grumpiness, why hadn't he aimed better?

When he really did it we were devastated. After that first try, the doctors had patched him up and sent him home, but it didn't heal properly. Infection set in. The pain became continuous. When he returned to the doctors, they diagnosed it as gangrene, with amputation of the leg being necessary.

During the afternoon proceeding the night he killed himself, I was off from work and at home. He came by from the doctor's office, but did not tell me what he'd been told. I learned later that they'd wanted to amputate his leg. At my house he started to drink, heavily. I had an appointment to do a reading and I asked him to leave. He hugged and kissed me and said, "I'll see you in the morning." I wondered why he'd said that. Had I promised to do something with him? I was not scheduled at work till noon.

That night, in the middle of the night, I got a phone call. It was a man's voice, but so garbled I did not recognize it as John's. I hung up. I thought it was an obscene phone caller as he was saying something that sounded like "baby...baby." After he hadn't been able to get me on the phone he called another lady friend to be on the line with him so he wouldn't have to die alone – at least. This is what we surmised later. She'd been able to understand what he was saying and he told her the doctor's grim news about his leg. Then he just said, "Goodbye," and she heard the gun go off. She immediately called the police and they found him dead. He'd just wanted a lady friend to be with him at his end. Poor, lonely, tortured man.

Two nights later he made good on his promise to let me know he was alive on the next plane. I woke up in the darkest part of the night to find my left hand being pulled on with such force that I was terrified. My hand was held was up in the air over me and I was being pulled upright out of my bed. I could see no one in my dimly lit bedroom. Instinctively, I realized that it was not human. I was ice cold. I screamed. The pulling continued. I did not think of my friend at that moment. Finally, being out from under the covers and partly out of the bed, in a panic, I thought to yell, "Let me go in the name of the Christ-consciousness!"

I was instantly dropped back into bed. I switched on a lamp. I was wet with sweat and shaking. My mouth was bone-dry. What hideous devil had come to me from between worlds? What or whom had come through the "doorway?"

I stayed up for a while, composing myself. Then, hoping to sleep once more I turned to put the lamp off and I saw, on the wall, a Picasso print my friend John had given me. It was hanging from its wire at a forty-five degree angle and was upside down. Now I knew it had been my friend who'd visited me and pulled on me. He'd always told me he loved me! Why tug on me with such strength and malevolence? I laid in the heavy darkness many hours pondering our strange relationship.

In the morning I called Susy, a member of the Association for Research and Enlightenment (ARE), the Edgar Cayce group. We worried that he was trapped in between worlds and might become earthbound, a ghost. I told her I'd taken pictures of my bruised hand and the upside-down picture that morning. My hand actually was very sore and turning purple. She was having an ARE meeting at her house that very night and promised to have the group try and contact John.

A day later she reported that they had been successful in contacting him. They asked him why he'd taken such a final step – his own life. He said he did not want to live with just one leg. Until then I did not know about the diagnosis. That was later confirmed by his other girlfriend who was on the phone with him when he died. John promised the group that he would not frighten me again, that he'd only wanted me to come with him. Yes, I'd felt that if that force had been successful in pulling my body out of bed, I would have been dead. I would have been found dead of a heart attack or stroke. Seems he thought so too. I loved him dearly, as a friend, but he was always a self-centered ladies' man. Surviving those long years in a prison camp would give one the excuse. And for him to feel the ultimate freedom that being out of the body gives to a person, it must have been the utmost joy for him. No steel leg-brace to slow him down, astounding! He probably wanted me to experience that freedom with him. I'd told him about my being out of the body. He thought I'd understand. We had done so many things together for several years now. We spoke the same language, all our own. He just wanted to have me with him.

A month later another close girlfriend who had been a member of our own Rat Pack, finally got up the nerve to tell me of her horrifying night-time visitor who tried to pull her out of her bed. She saw enough of him to realize it was John. Comparing notes we found it had been the same night – two nights after his suicide. She was still upset, with no explanation until I brought her up to date and told her not to worry, he wouldn't try that again. He'd promised ARE not to bother us. She'd been frightened to go to sleep each night, afraid he would be back to grab at her again. We talked about how sad it was for families to have the heartache of believing suicides went straight to Hell. We certainly had proof that didn't happen in his case.

The God I know draws back into himself ALL of his beloved children. My God is LOVE. This man had been through a real Hell here on earth, the Japanese prison. Now he was with the Father. John has come to visit me many times in these twenty years since, but never as that frightening, strong ghost that he was two days after he died. He made his transition with the help of the ARE that night and is at peace.

Chapter 7

Controlling the Weather

Psychic phenomenon is not yet reliable. The T.V. series *Medium* has come closest, in my opinion, at describing how the psychic world works. Clues for Allison Dubois, the series' psychic, come to her in dreams – one way to access information – in bits and pieces. This is so true for me. In the J.B. Rhine studies this was the outstanding problem. Nothing unfolds like a novel, with one portion following another to form an understandable picture. Frustrating!

I am not troubled by this piecemeal information process, and I am just happy when I receive the bits and pieces. I enjoy the puzzle, the need to figure them out – it is an adventure. I have come to the understanding that it is meant to be this way until we have evolved into a better state of acceptance. In my own case I have accomplished some startling things. But, if I could reproduce these phenomenon on demand, would I become too self-important? I think, most assuredly. With the writing of this book I realize why I have never told many friends about my experiences. The stories chosen for this book are only a slice of the pie. If even my own family knew that I am possibly capable of creating a situation – for example, a sunny day when rain was a certainty – they might come to blame me when bad things happen in their lives. Would they ever believe that I might "put a spell" on them? Think of the imbalance of power in a family that could cause!

Through the centuries, over and over, this has happened to good, well-meaning psychics. When the church officials felt they were losing control because people were learning to read and began to recognize they had spiritual gifts outside of church rules, the priests were thrown into a panic. A lot of money was involved with their losing collections at every service. Can we not visualize the many council meetings, the heated discussions, and the discourse behind locked doors? Something had to be done! The common man was learning to read and think for himself. So from the top came down the decree – oppression.

The world fell into the man-made age of the inquisition. The dark ages returned.

In our country, even, we had another dark age in Salem, Massachusetts. While the dark age of the Inquisition had at its center "witchcraft," the horror of Salem was completely about witches. It was 1692 and the story is well known. Now it is believed that the whole tragic affair was probably caused by some hysterical teenaged girls who had been listening to tales of Voodoo told to them by a black maid from Barbados. It was Colonial America during the Puritan Age. More than two hundred people were accused of practicing witchcraft and over 20 were executed. It is believed that at least thirty-four people died as a result of the injustices.

I am lucky to have lived in our present age. Once again we are free to use our spiritual gifts to benefit each other. However, even today, we need to use discretion. Challenging the status quo possesses some danger even in our liberated day. People still fear what they do not understand.

The healings that I have done, and not talked about, have faded in my mind to the point of me thinking that perhaps the results would have happened without my doing anything. It's easy to assume that I might only have been dreaming. BUT I KNOW I WAS NOT, and then there are my diaries with my evidence.

The Big Rain

The desire to control our weather, rain in particular, with some kind of mental or psychic power must be as old as humanity itself. One can understand why the ancients considered the weather as Gods. It colors our days in so many ways.

Skeptics would call a successful production of rain a mere coincidence, but a hurricane turned into a placid breeze, forget it! I've done both. Jesus stopped the winds and calmed the waters. He promised us that the things he did we also could do, and even more.

We have all read about people who can cause a large, heavy wooden table to levitate. Some of us have seen this feat performed. I have. Then why would we find it hard to believe that one could influence the billions of ions within a cloud to produce rain? I felt that I could do just that after reading about how to do it in a book by Jess Stearn – the popular author of several books and a personal friend of my friend Maya Perez.

The first time I was determined to make it rain, and was half way there by my believing I could, I had promised a boyfriend that it would happen in three days because I wanted to see him again. I had one of those major crushes on this boot-scootin' cowboy. He was in the business, besides raising quarter horses, of cutting hay. He'd told me he couldn't see me until it rained, at which time he couldn't spend the night cutting hay because the hay would be wet.

One technique from Mr. Stearn was to concentrate on a particular cloud seen in the sky and to mentally ascend into that cloud. Then when one feels one is a part of that very cloud, feel it and see it breaking up and falling to the earth as rain. I'd given myself three days. By the third day of following his method I was dreaming clouds in my sleep, feeling them in my very pores, and pour it did!

At the furniture store where I worked with my former boyfriend, John, I shared what I was attempting to do. Since we worked together he was with me when we began to hear the thunder and lightning. He was even more excited than I was. Then the rain poured from the sky in torrential buckets. He told the whole store I was making it rain. Most believed it as he had also told them a lot about me.

John pointed out that I had gone overboard! There was no need to produce such a violent storm when the weatherman had predicted there was no chance of rain. This 'stunt' of mine made me ill!

I'd used up so much energy in this my first try at controlling the weather, I was as exhausted as if I had run a marathon and had to miss work the next day. I am sure the confrontation that night with the boyfriend didn't help matters either. It was still raining in the dry month of June when the first crop of hay was usually harvested.

"What in the hell are you?" he yelled at me when I opened the door. He was wet, but he wouldn't come in. He was afraid of me and he was livid! He left, and I never saw him again.

Several months later I heard from my former Mind Control teacher who had, by chance, met my hay-baler cowboy at a bar and had talked about mind control. My farmer friend asked him if it was possible for a person to make it rain, explaining he had this girlfriend who told him she would make it rain in three days and she did even though we'd been in a drought. "You must mean June," my teacher said. My teacher told him he'd also seen me do similar feats. Lover boy never came back; I'd lost him. I never heard from him after that night that he was at my door in the rain. More the pity for him. When I look at my face in the mirror these days I see a lot of lines. A couple of them were put there by him. Don't ask for what you can't handle.

More Rain

In controlling rain, on occasion I have also stopped a predicted rain from falling on my granddaughter's and grandson's birthday parties. Often, as soon as the little guests had all departed it would begin to rain again as scheduled. My granddaughter's in her thirties now and has birthday parties for her own child. She still calls and requests, "Grand-Mama, please don't let it rain tomorrow." Sometimes it's just for a picnic of the family that she requests a day of sunshine.

Protection from the Forces of Nature - Humbling

The Texas coast has frequent hurricanes and warnings of hurricanes. An especially fierce one was Carla during the fall of 1970. When we heard the alert that they were evacuating the populace of Corpus Christi; a girlfriend and fellow salesperson became frantic. Her two young children were visiting her sister in Corpus. Her house was right on the beach and the backyard had turned into ocean, just beyond the sea wall. She was refusing to leave her house! The sister claimed she'd weathered many a hurricane with no problems. The big problem was she had my friend's young children, a boy and a girl, with her. This storm was a class four hurricane and was headed right towards Corpus Christi! Only fool-hearty people would ignore the warning to evacuate. All the yelling and screaming from this end was ignored and she stayed.

Most of us believe we are invincible. Her sister qualified as a charter member of that club. My coworker couldn't work. She paced the furniture floor. She cried in the lunchroom. Several of us joined her there to pray for her children. I wanted to help. I'd had success with the weather many times, but only small stuff. How could I take on a hurricane?

I went off by myself and meditated, trying to find a solution. "Don't fight the storm ... protect the house!" I heard.

It was about two days before telephone lines were back up and her sister could call. She was so apologetic, saying she had no idea the storm was going to be that bad. (What about all the warnings?) All was well at her house. It was the only one on her street still intact, undamaged. All around her houses were simply gone, blown away. She said it was as if an iron wall had been erected around her property. She was told that that was exactly what I'd done, mentally, to protect them.

My work hadn't helped my friend to be at peace or to be able to sleep but it had had the desired effect. Thank you, higher consciousness.

This process did not produce illness in me, though I would have done it anyway, nor has it happened again. But nothing I've done since had been as intense as that first try at the rain.

Once More with Feeling – No Rain

Every November, John Randolph and Jan Price conducted the "Mystery School" in Boerne, Texas. It's was a gathering of Quartus members, and similar thinking adults, to study the Ancient Mysteries.

One November, the morning of our final session, it was raining ALL those cats and dogs we hear about. The meeting room was across a courtyard from our rooms. The sixty-five participants had to run through the rain with umbrellas and newspapers over our heads to attend the final morning session. The skies were laden and the weather channel had predicted a daylong soaker.

John Price said to me, "June, we need you to stop this rain long enough for us to load our cars and get on the road so we can get home safely." I love a challenge! Just as we all hugged each other with our goodbyes the rain ceased. An hour later the last car was packed, we had all checked out, and were driving out of the valley from our hotel at Tapatio Springs when the rain, once again, came down in Texas-sized buckets.

Chapter 8

Manifestations

We all have unknown, untapped powers that would be awesome to behold if we would just open up to them. A few times in my life, a window has opened up for me on the hitherto unrealized promise that Jesus left with us: John 14:12 , "He that believeth in Me, the works that I do shall he do also, and greater works than these shall he do; because I go to the Father." As the kids say, "Awesome!"

The Salmon Story

The definition of manifest: to make clear or obvious to the eye or mind. The definition of manifestation: the action or fact or showing an abstract idea, a symptom of an ailment, a version of incarnation of something or someone, an appearance of a ghost or spirit. ("manifest &

manifestation." Oxford Dictionaries. Online Edition. 2013.) I had a priceless best friend named Dee in my life for a brief twelve years. I've written of him earlier. He was my friend from Oklahoma. When we were together we had several amazing manifestation experiences. I believe it was caused by our combined energies.

Once, when we walked toward each other, a current of bright blue electricity sparked between us for about two feet in length. We were at a party. People gasped. We were on a tile entryway floor, not on carpeting and not wearing wool.

The first time I drove with Dee to visit his birthplace in Oklahoma, we stayed at the home of his Norwegian friend, Helmute, owner of a beauty salon. Helmute was a gourmet cook. He had invited another couple, plus a single "friend," to have dinner with us on Saturday night. Saturday morning Helmute hurried us out the door so he could have the day alone to prepare for his dinner party. We agreed to go by his fish market and pick up six fresh salmon steaks he'd ordered. He asked that we be back by 5:30 that evening, guests were arriving at 6:30.

At 5:00 that evening we were in downtown Oklahoma City. We'd done the cowboy museum and several other points of interest and were having an ice cream at Dee's favorite childhood drugstore, still in operation with its soda fountain. We noticed the clock over the prescription counter and were horrified to see the time had slipped away from us. We hadn't picked up the fish! We were thirty minutes away from the fish market in Nichol's Hills and on Saturdays it closed at 5:00 pm. We were panicked. There seemed nothing we could do, but go back to Helmute and face the music, very ugly music we feared. I was near tears.

Oklahoma City grocery stores in the seventies did not sell fresh salmon steaks. We regretted that the least we could have done was tend to the small task our generous host had entrusted to us. So we were in a black mood as we drove toward his house.

Three blocks before we arrived there we joyfully, gratefully spied a fish market! It was in the corner of a strip center at an intersection and it was OPEN! This was a spotless black and white tile place, very New York style, all chrome and glass. A very friendly, attentive butcher packaged up for us six beautiful, thick Alaskan salmon steaks in white butcher paper. The price seemed unusually low. We thanked him for being open. "Always open for you," he answered. We thanked him a second time and hurried out. We were only running fifteen minutes late. THEN, the miracle! We were so relieved and grateful that this shop was still open that it wasn't until later when we compared notes, we realized there were no other customers.

The salmon was a hit with our friend, the cook. "Very fresh!" he exclaimed. He inquired as to where we'd purchased them, as his butcher did not use white paper. We then had to confess our crime and we described the market we'd found three blocks away. "No, no," Helmute said, "There is no fish market in this whole area." He vowed we were mistaken. When the others guests arrived, all talk of it ceased. But we knew we'd found this fish market in that strip center. I still remember that salmon for all these thirty years. It was divine. Everyone praised the cook. He, humbly, gave credit to the fish itself.

The next morning, to prove ourselves wrong, we drove back to the shopping center. "See," said Helmute, "No fish market." Yes, there was the same row of shops, but no market... never was, or has been since, a fish in that intersection. A Walgreen's, an insurance office, a dress shop, and in the corner, a florist! Had we been drinking? No, just eating ice cream. Had we been in the twilight zone? Perhaps. We had certainly needed help, desperately. That morning we drove for many blocks in all directions to find only residences. Could we have gotten help from a divine source? Absolutely!

Next, what else have I manifested out of thin air? This time it was by myself – for myself.

A Manifestation

My second husband and I had been driving a rental car while ours was being repaired. In the car were our suitcases and purchases from a trip we'd made by car over the weekend. I had bought a pair of pretty navy pumps for myself to match a new outfit. We turned in the rent car after transferring everything into our car. When we reached home and unloaded, I did not have my shoes.

We called the car rental office. They looked in the car we'd turned in and found no shoes. We even stopped by the rental place the next day to see if possibly they'd been found. The car was not there; it had been rented. No shoes in their lost and found. I was distraught. I loved those shoes! I am hard to fit and have a difficult time finding comfortable dress shoes. Those had felt like they would need no breaking in.

Two days later, there were THOSE shoes in the distinctive pink box on my closet's top-most shelf. I did not keep shoes up there. Had I accidentally put that box on the top shelf? No way! My husband confirmed that. He carried everything into the house that day we came home. He knew he had not put that box there. He NEVER put a thing away. And there was nobody else. Out of my deep desire to have those shoes, did I manifest them from wherever they had been left? The

Twilight Zone? No! My own divine source? I think so!

Another Manifestation

One of the treasured items I kept from my mother's estate was her old iron treadle, Singer night stand for the guest room with the addition of a glass top. These old machines and their bases are prized items in antique shops, bringing big bucks.

We put it, temporarily, alongside the garage, under the overhang, as there was "no room in the inn." Our garage was a crammed-full disaster. We knew rain would not harm the base to any great extent, as it was already rusty. It had been outside at Mother's as a plant stand. We put it out of sight of our street. One would have to be prowling to find it. There was an old bicycle leaning against it also awaiting paint. I did not think of theft. Who but an antique dealer could envision a use for it?

My husband had to spend a month in the hospital. I never left him, precious man. On our first night home, while I was meditating, I had a vision. I saw a man and a woman carrying my sewing machine base away. In the morning when I went out to get the daily newspaper, I checked the side of the garage. The bicycle that had been leaning on the base was lying tossed down on its side and the sewing machine base was gone. I was furious. My vision had been true.

I complained to the universe, loudly! I NEVER lose anything. I am never robbed. All I have belongs to the Universe and will be here after I'm gone. While I am here it is under my care and will remain with me. That machine was my treasure, left to me by my mother. I had seen it all my life, and love it. I still see in my memory; my mother, bent over it late at night, finishing a dress for me to wear on an occasion the following day.

This had been my mother's first Singer. Seldom did a day go by that she didn't sew. There were six of us and she even made our pajamas. I often went to sleep hearing the whir of the machine. She ironed every seam so my clothes never looked homemade. She copied clothes out of the latest fashion magazines. She did jeweled necklines and ruffles, Peter Pan collars and wide velvet sashes. I even had appliquéd bodices and my brothers had sailor suits and dress-suits for church.

It was probably the most exciting day of her life when she brought home her new electric Singer machine and the old Treadle went into storage. She never threw anything away.

She taught me to sew when I was a teenager and I did the same with my daughter. Her mother always sewed, so this thread ran down through the generations. The loss of this family relic was traumatic.

Out of great pain can come great strength, so over a two-week period I envisioned my base back where it belonged, under the eave of the garage. I forgave the people who took it – very important, this business of forgiveness, but it must be genuine. Then to my shock – it is difficult to believe in our power – there it was, not alongside the garage, but under the Chinese Pistachio tree in front of the garage. Did the thieves bring it back? I'll never believe that. I KNOW I manifested it in my certainty that it was mine. I love thinking of the man and woman that I saw removing it, and who are now puzzled by its disappearance, perhaps from a locked warehouse.

Manifesting Gasoline

My best girlfriend and I drove to Steamboat Springs, Colorado, to ski. We had a lovely condo overlooking several snowy slopes, crowded with skiers from dawn till dusk. I had never skied; and after one lesson of sliding down the baby slope on my ass-clad, new, expensive, winter resort britches, I was ready to give up those unfriendly, long narrow pieces of wood that nature had not planned on for my feet.

I enjoyed waiting for my friend while she attacked the high slopes. I was content to watch her endanger her arms and legs. Meanwhile I was drinking hot buttered rum and ogling the handsome men by the massive stone fireplace in the lodge at the base of a ski lift.

After days of this inaction on my part, she suggested we drive to Jackson Hole, Wyoming, for a day of sightseeing. I was delighted. The scenery along that route through the mountains was splendiferous in the morning light. I oohed and aahed, and she laughed at me.

I fell in love with the mountain town of Jackson Hole, an artist's paradise. This trip was in the seventies so the town was still somewhat undiscovered by most tourists, especially in the winter. The shops were filled with interesting things. We bought tee shirts and scarves. We had lunch. We shopped again. We found a western-themed bar with fine-looking drug-store cowboys, and before we realized it, the daylight was fading and we'd whizzed away our chance for getting back through the snow-covered mountains before dark. And more important, we'd forgotten to buy gas! We didn't remember that fact until we were on our way.

We were high up on the narrow mountain road, snow towering on each side of the undivided highway, when we realized we had not filled up the gas tank in town. From here on, there would be no towns, no gas stations, no houses, nothing but fresh snow that had started to fall. We were a bit more than half way to Steamboat so turning around, while impossible anyway, was not an option. Now, with snow hindering our progress, we were in trouble.

This friend was also a Mind Control graduate. When staring at the gas gauge hovering at the empty line could not change the reading, we decided to work together to mentally fill the tank. I reminded her that it works better with two people doing it together. (She knew this as truth as she was the friend who helped me to cause impotency of my faithless boyfriend, John.) We had the confidence that we could produce the fuel we needed to get home. So we concentrated on "GAS, GASOLINE, FUEL!"

When two foolish, half-intoxicated women start a dark journey over narrow mountain passes they have enough strikes against them. But, we weren't through dealing with bad luck yet. A car passed us, driven by a man. He hit a large rock that flew up and crashed into our windshield. He looked back, but didn't even slow down. On the driver's side the rock shattered the glass! We zigzagged for a moment until my friend gained control and leveled off safely on our side of the highway. Now she had to peer between cracks for her visibility while the cold and the snow rushed in and bit into her face.

We cursed him for a while, but really wanted the snow to stop falling – mostly into our window. Then we discussed . . . what if the *manifesting* DIDN'T work for us? Ann, who usually prepares for lengthy stays on snow-covered mountains with her blankets, extra water, and extra food, had not thought about it for this trip and we laughed, and cried, about that mishap.

"Lovely gas, beautiful gas – flowing into our tank and filling it!"

I joined her and we continued our mantra until we saw the resplendent, shining lights of Steamboat Springs in front of us. The IMPOSSIBLE DREAM – we had MADE it! Not on a wing and a prayer – on a mantra and a prayer. We were so grateful; we forgot to ask the service station attendant why he'd been open at all, and especially this late. The gas ticket at the service station showed the exact amount of gas that her tank would hold. We hadn't produced actual gas with our manifesting, just the results.

We were too wound up to sleep. We both love to cook and we had a fridge full of food as we had shopped, but never eaten at the apartment, preferring the lodge with the giant fireplace. We cooked ourselves a repast and fell into bed at midnight with full tummies and grateful hearts that we'd been able to manifest ourselves to safety.

A Blown Tire

During second husband Sam's final year, we were on our way to his chemo treatment when our tire blew out as we drove through the underpass that led to the main highway. I was frustrated as I realized he could not possibly help me change the tire. I doubted I could accomplish such a feat, as I had never done it before. To add to that, it was over ninety degrees outside; very, very hot!

But, I knew I had to try. First, I put my head down on the steering wheel and silently declared that I needed an angel, quickly! I raised my head to see a truck pulling up in back of us. I got out and greeted a young man getting out of the truck wearing, among other things, cowboy boots and a cowboy hat. Obviously, he saw that we were in trouble and had stopped to help. I didn't see where he had come from.

"Ma'am, my momma would beat me with a switch, old as I am, if I didn't change you-all's tire!" the cowboy shouted to me as he jumped out of his truck. Perhaps he was just a passing neighbor with a kind heart, or like a Della Reese character in *Touched by an Angel,* I had manifested an angel dressed in cowboy clothes. In any case, he WAS a tire-changing angel and we were on our way.

Chapter 9

Ouija Boards

I am not fond of Ouija Boards. In fact, I find it impossible to endorse the use of them. The most common explanation of how they work is that one's own subconscious comes through one's hands to spell out answers or messages. Our subconscious minds can harbor some very dark thoughts, all unknown to our conscious minds – things that would surely horrify us.

My first experience with the Ouija board was as a gag-gift that I was given and immediately shelved! I was not interested in it. I'd never even removed the plastic wrapping. I'd often read warnings of them and been told by friends that they were evil – of the devil. So there it stayed for years, on a shelf, hiding under a jigsaw puzzle, in a box the same size, like a brown recluse spider waiting to pounce.

My friend, Dee, was spending the night with me. (Dee is the friend with whom I share powerful psychic energy.) We'd shared a whole bottle of Shiraz when he talked me into trying our luck on that long-unused gift. I actually had some trouble locating it, but as soon as I did he opened it and set it up on my dining room table. I was extremely wary and I lit a candle for its protective vapors.

We placed our hands on the planchette and it almost immediately began to move in circles. We stared at each other in awe. Each of us carefully took our hands off one at a time. Even with just the one person's hand it continued to move in circles. We convinced ourselves that we were not controlling it, only giving it our energy. It seemed to be circling, as if waiting for something from us. We asked for a name. To our wonder, it spelled out R-U-T-H. We next asked if there was a message for us. Yes, "A death for Jack Coulter, October the fifteenth." I nearly screamed. This was my ex-husband's name! The fifteenth was the next day!

I sprang up from the table and called my daughter. She, also, became upset and promised to find her dad and tell him. Soon I had a call back. She had found him. His reply was, "Tell the Soothsayer (always a smart-ass), I will be okay. I'm not going on my usual Saturday morning fishing trip. I'll be with my girlfriend the rest of the day. She's in the hospital." So, I settled down as best I could but that was the end of our experimenting for the night.

The next morning when I came into work one of the salesmen said, "Was that your ex-husband or a relative who was found dead in the Trinity River last night?" I grabbed for support on the nearest piece of furniture, my heart racing. My pulse rate must have hit the rooftop as I reached for the newspaper in his hand. Co-workers said I turned snow-white and someone helped me to a chair. My ex might have been the butt of all my sour grapes jokes, but deep down I still felt that ole feelin.' I read the front page. The body in the river was that of my ex's brother. He'd been found floating close to shore.

It was hard to concentrate on selling furniture that day. I had liked this brother-in-law a lot. He was the family's black sheep, but was always a charmer. He was black-haired, brown eyed, with perfect features. He had always reminded me of Clark Gable. He was, to some of us, even more handsome than Clark Gable. Divorced, with four children in another state, he had been a heavy drinker for years. I hadn't seen him in months and so, that day, I mourned for a handsome man gone too soon. I came to the realization, mid-day, that the *Ruth* on the Ouija board had said, "a death FOR, not a death OF." Amazing!

That night I was home alone. I kept staring at the board; it was still set up on my dining room table. Could I work it by myself? Well, it had moved last night when we tried with just one of us on the planchette. It was late at night. I was not comfortable with it anyway – as if it were alive. And what would I do if I became frightened? Who could I call? Could I call Dee? Of course.

"So – okay, girl," I said to myself, "'Faint heart ne'er won...!" The movies are full of that girl who goes out in the dark, or into that dark room alone, and we always cry, "No! No!" and then feel she deserved to die because she acted so stupidly.

I gathered my little bit of courage, lit a candle, sat down and put two fingers on the planchette. It immediately started to move in circles. I turned ice cold, but I couldn't stop. I was fascinated. I asked it to identify itself. It spelled out, "Ruth." Before I could voice another question the planchette flew into circles, and then settled into pointing out letters. I used my left hand only, while my right hand wrote down the letters... "A deed most foul hath woman seen... murder... murder..." – then nothing. I needed a friend! I was alone, thirty miles into the country north of Dallas, and six blocks from the nearest neighbor. I went to bed and, child-like, hid completely under the covers sleeping fitfully until I could see daylight.

When I talked with my ex-husband the next day, he told me that the forensic scientist had determined that his brother had been murdered, and was dead before being dumped into the water. This confirmed for me that what I'd been told on the board was a truth. I told him about the message claiming there was a woman involved. My ex reported that his brother had been living in a drifter's shack along the river with a woman. They were both perceived to be heavy drinkers by the street people interviewed. When the police questioned the woman she denied having any knowledge of foul play. After a couple of weeks the police dropped their investigation for lack of evidence. Loving relatives were not willing to give up, but the authorities could not justify further work on what they deemed "street people." There is no justice if you are indigent.

The Ouija board had tried its best to help us, and it proven to me that it actually does work, though it has caused me some sleepless nights and needless worries. Only once more did my friend Dee and I sit down with the board. Once again we contacted "Ruth." She spelled out that she wanted to dictate a book to me about Russia. Immediately, I felt a cold, oppressive shudder and knew that this was something I should not do. I put my board away back into its box, on the high shelf under a jigsaw puzzle. I still have it and I also have my notes from those nights, but I like to think it is because like my mother, I am a person who seldom tosses anything.

Ruth

Several weeks later I was at a party at my friend Naoma's house. I did not know that her teenager had a Ouija board in her room until a young girl came into the living area and loudly asked, "Is there someone here who knows a Ruth? She's on the Ouija board and wants to talk to the person who's going to write her book about Russia." Whoa! I didn't respond.

It ruined my evening. What was this thing with Ruth? Why was she so insistent on writing this book? Was she someone from the other side desperate to write a book she's been planning until an unexpected death brought an end to those plans? Why was it so important for me to be the one to write it? Was it me from another life? I have always wanted to write. (Considering Ruth's desperation, I'd better get this book written before I have to leave!)

Through the years, I have been called "Ruth" by a large number of people since this happened, and I've corrected them, as it sends a chill through me. I admit I don't know what this means. Unfinished business from a past life? Karma? Perhaps.

A Taipei Witch

On the subject of Ouija boards, the best example I can provide for the fact that they can invite trouble – evil – into a house are the terrifying events that happened to my granddaughter and her husband.

They operated and owned an English language school in Taipei, Taiwan. They lived in a small, rented house near their school. Four other American friends lived nearby – these friends had a Ouija board. She knew how I felt about boards and had told her husband to have nothing to do with them if their friends were using it.

One evening, he had a bone-chilling event happen to him in their bedroom. He was alone, sitting on the bed when he saw what he thought was a wolf leap up beside him onto the bed. He was aware that it was not alive because it was an indistinct gray fog that he could see through even though it was dense. It slinked across the bed while he watched in fear as it turned into a black woman. His next thought was, "What is a black woman doing in Asia?" She was slim with black, short hair – she reminded him of the actress Eartha Kitt. She crouched across the bed only three feet away and glowered at him. Then she was gone. The air in the room was awful, thick and cold, radiating despair. He sat still, unable to move or do anything for a while. Finally, he slept.

The next night she was back, repeating her actions once again. On this second visit, he asked her for her name and age. He heard her in his head and on a piece of paper he wrote, *Susan* and *23*. He did not tell my granddaughter about either incident, as he had no explanation for what he had seen and felt that it might scare her.

When my granddaughter was gone for two weeks to visit her parents in the states, he invited his Ouija board friends to come and set up in his bedroom. He invited them to call for the spirit who lived in the bedroom. There was no doubt about who came on the board. Right away she spelled out "Susan." Then, to the question of age she indicated the number 23. My grandson did not work the board because he had promised his wife he never would. His buddy Chris, who was on the planchette, seemed to incur the spirit's wrath and she cursed him in between telling his buddies that she had been murdered in this room. She described how she'd been dressed and gave them the details of her death from a brutal stabbing with blood finally covering every inch of her lifeless body.

It frightened all of them. They stopped their questions and put the board away, but could talk of nothing else. They were shocked when my grandson-in-law showed them what he had written down on paper that night she visited him. Then, he told them the story of the luminous wolf that had leaped on his bed.

After a few more drinks they gained the courage to contact Susan again. Two of the men, who hadn't tried it before, begged to be the ones with the planchette this time. There was a lot of nervous laughter. The men had turned into small boys. My grandson-in-law forgot about his wife's warnings – while the cat's away, boys will be boys.

The two men instantly contacted with the spirit of the murdered woman. This time, my grandson-in-law was the one with the paper and pen, again feeling like he was not doing Ouija since he was not hands-on. Susan went crazy, rapidly spelling out obscenities directed at Chris, telling him to, "go f - - - himself." The language became more and more course. At first the men were laughing, but the laughing did not last long. When the verbiage made no sense at all they gave up.

When my granddaughter returned to Taipei, she immediately knew something was wrong; there's a lot of her grandmother in her psyche. She felt a cold blast on entering the house. In the master bedroom it was worse. It felt like walking into a refrigerator. Her husband admitted what he had done, blaming it on his friends, of course. He confessed he had been sleeping in the living room because he was frightened by the atmosphere in their bedroom. Their two Chinese Shar Pei dogs would not go into the bedroom at all and were spending a lot of time whining.

My loved ones tried to sleep in their bedroom now that there were two of them. They huddled under extra blankets, only to awaken in a cold sweat. They were both having nightmares. Twice, my granddaughter actually saw the murdered black woman. She had materialized in the darkness in wispy, glowing fogs. She glared at her with hate, shook her fist and came towards my granddaughter in a threatening manner. When my granddaughter would scream, the woman would fade away. The Ouija Board had given her heinous spirit strength and more access to the room where she'd been murdered, and she seemed to be bent on revenge. Soon they could bear the woman no longer and they moved to new quarters.

When my grandson-in-law told me of this experience he also said he'd had other frightening, unexplainable things happen. He is somewhat a believer in psychic occurrences and in my family it grows stronger with all of us through the years.

He told me that when he was about ten years old he was with his parents in Egypt. They were visiting the great pyramid in Cairo and he saw several spirits dancing around the top of the great pyramid. He did not tell anyone for fear that he would not be believed. Later, his older brother looked over at him and exclaimed, "I thought you were dead!"

"Why did you think I was dead?"

"Well, I saw you dancing way up in the sky around the big pyramid and I could see right through you, so I thought you were dead."

I cannot explain this except that it could have been that his ethereal body left to dance with the souls he saw having fun on high. At any rate, it's interesting.

Advice

Indiscriminate use of the Ouija Board is always dangerous, especially combined with drugs or alcohol as these substances render us relaxed enough to become victims of possession. The thought of an incarnate soul taking over one's personality is the ultimate in scary stories in the occult world. The take-over process can be so subtle that if one is not aware, he or she can unintentionally invite in an unwelcome, even evil, spirit. No one is possessed without offering, albeit unknowingly, an opening. Marijuana users are an example of offering an opening (more about this in Chapter 10). So while this subject of the Ouija Board seems fascinating, it is a vast area of phenomena that should NOT be used as a toy.

Chapter 10

UFO's & ET's
(Unidentified Flying Objects & Extraterrestrials)

"I've never seen a little green man.
I never hope to see one.
But I can surely tell you this,
I'd rather see than be one!"

Or was that verse originally about a "Purple Cow" by Gelett Burgess (1866-1951), that first appeared in 1895 in the first issue of *The Lark*, a humor magazine. It is a frequently quoted poem, often used in parody, and was the poem Burgess would spend much of his life trying to surpass. In *The Lark*, it was an illustrated four line poem that it goes like this: "I never saw a purple cow / I never hope to see one; / But I can tell you, anyhow, / I'd rather see than be one!" (1-4).

Nevertheless, its essence is timeless and sums up my feelings on the subject of flying saucers. There have been rumors of visitors from outer space since time began. These stories have made it into our history books – some even believe there are stories of them in the Bible. I don't know what to believe, even with some frightening evidence of my own. I find it an interesting subject, though disconcerting; thus, I remain ambivalent.

My Personal Communion

I spent my high school years in San Antonio, Texas, where the novelist Whitley Strieber also grew up. When I read several of his books, especially *Communion,* I was haunted by a strange memory from a night when I was living on the shores of Lake Dallas.

I awoke that morning in a cold sweat with shadowy memories of *something* having happened to me in the night. I felt violated and somehow soiled. I've never been raped, but I thought I must be having a similar reaction. I wanted to cry. I had feelings of blackness and something akin to a memory of devils or creepy-like insects in my room. My eyes were sensitive to light as if I'd been staring into a bright, overhead light-fixture. All that day I was on the verge of tears, even crying at the smallest difficulty. My left arm hurt, but it was another whole day before I discovered a two-inch wide and deep depression in my skin above my wrist. There was no scar, just a curious deep depression, still visible there now, though not as deep as it was then.

I had no clear memory or understanding of why I felt such sadness. Later when I read Strieber's books a light turned on in my brain and I've wondered if UFOs were a possible explanation. I did live in an isolated area with no close neighbors. Perhaps I was abducted for several hours while they removed tissue from my arm. Perhaps they wanted a piece of me, being a psychic, like those Oklahoma witches had wanted some of my blood. UFOs had been reported being sighted several times around Lake Dallas, close to where I lived.

Yes, I have to smile at the absurdity of my lack of understanding. Shouldn't a psychic know what happened? It's illogical and preposterous, even comical, that I haven't much of a clue. I had a phone call, once, from a man wanting to book a reading with me. When I asked for his name, he said, "You should be able to tell me if you're such a good psychic." I told him to get real. He hung up on me.

And now we have these cattle mutilations. It would appear that the ET's are using animals for their studies of our world. After all, we humans also use animals in our scientific studies; even people – prisoners for example.

It's interesting to me that Whitley Strieber has changed his mind more than once, from his first book through his latest, on the nature of ET's. There are many other hypotheses about whom or what is visiting us from space or from a parallel world. One can pick up a dozen different books on this subject at any bookstore.

UFO's

In a curious tie-in to Lake Dallas and UFOs, a shocking and disturbing thing occurred a few years later. I was living back in the city and had met a young, pretty Hispanic girl, brown eyed, dark haired, slightly built and always smiling. She had come to me for a reading and became a friend. Her parents owned a beauty shop. She had a brother and a sister, also beauticians, who worked together with their mother in this salon. She found me through a client who was a close friend of mine.

This stylist was the kind of bouncy, cheerful girl that one likes to invite to a party. Who doesn't want a pretty twenty-year-old at their party? So that year I'd invited her to a birthday party my daughter was giving for me. (I still have snap-shots I treasure from that evening.) Everyone loved her. She was that kind of girl.

I read for her several times that summer, the usual problems with boyfriends, her parents, or problems with customers at the beauty salon. She always seemed very practical.

About two weeks before Thanksgiving she called wanting to see me, not for a reading but on a matter personal for me. Over a glass of wine she told me a story. I'll admit, accustomed as I was to hearing weird tales, this took some trust in her for me to believe. She said she'd been alone in her apartment, her roommate out for the evening. Suddenly, a woman appeared in front of her and said she was a spokesperson for some visitors from outer space who would like for her to bring her friend, June the Psychic, to this particular spot on Lake Dallas where a space craft was scheduled to land at 10:00 p.m., two weeks from then. After delivering that message the figure had dissolved before her eyes.

I wondered what high-quality marijuana, or substance, she'd been smoking. I asked her and she insisted she'd had nothing until the wine we'd been sharing. I told her most adamantly that I had no interest in the subject of flying saucers and ET's or her friends playing pranks. I even agreed that perhaps UFO's were a true phenomenon, but I dealt with enough weird stuff in my life, daily, without adding little green men to the mix. She said the woman had stressed that it was highly important that I be there at 10:00 p.m., on that date. "Not to me," I replied. "It is highly important for my peace of mind that I decline!" She thought it would be exciting. I didn't. She said she'd drive. That was not a consideration for me. She left disappointed, but said she understood.

I believed that would be the end of it, but three more times she called me in the hope that I had changed my mind. Each time I felt like huge insects were all around me. If it had been a daylight meeting, it was possible I might have gone with her, but 10 p.m. at a deserted spot on the lake – FORGET IT! For many years I'd been subliminally haunted by a reading the gypsy-like psychic Bertie Catchings of Dallas, now deceased, had done for me. At this reading she immediately had picked up that I, too, was a reader, although not yet working as such. I would not start until a year later. She foretold that I soon would be giving a lot of readings, an accurate prediction. Then she warned me to always be very careful of where I went as she saw that I would be kidnapped by some powerful men who were serious investors in the stock market. She said they would only feed me when I made an accurate stock market prediction. Threaten me with ANYTHING but loss of food! For food, I'd sing like a bird! I tucked that info back in my brain where the cobwebs live. But, now it surfaced.

I began receiving daily calls that were coming from the hair stylist. Each time she seemed a little more anxious, more insistent. She told me the woman had returned again and again, more pertinacious each time, now turning ominous, this from my cute and cheerful client and friend.

Thanksgiving Eve she called on the phone reminding me that we were to go that next night. I had house guests; my son and his family, my mother and stepfather. She begged me to let her come over and talk. She was crying. I was so tired of her whining and I asked her, "What part of no do you not understand?"

My son and his wife are both mental health professionals. They were concerned that I might be dealing with a mentally ill person. She said the saucer people were going to kill her and her whole family if she could not produce me at the lake for them. I felt sorry for her, but I hung up.

The next day was Thanksgiving Day and she showed up at my door without calling. I was busy baking my tits over a hot stove for twelve people, so my son talked with her. He and his wife changed their opinion of her on meeting her in person. They diagnosed the girl as genuinely terrified. They saw raw fear in her eyes, hard to fake even for an accomplished actress, which she was not. She was crying hysterically. They judged that if she was making it up, she was unaware.

"They are really going to kill me and my whole family!" she screamed.

I had wondered from the start why the spirit who manifested in her apartment would not have appealed directly to me. Why torture a poor friend? She had asked this question herself and been told that I had too much protection around me for them to get through to me. This I knew to be true. I still have many angels protecting me.

That information, though, frightened me more. Why did I need to have all this protection if these 'creatures' meant me no harm?

My son dealt with her for me. It was Thanksgiving for gosh sakes! I had twelve people in the house for a three o'clock dinner. I was the cook. I felt so sorry for her, but I could not leave at nine that night to go out to the lake, an hour away, for this supposed saucer meeting.

Everyone was into her story by this time and felt sorry for her and they all wondered if she was on some heavy drug – except my son who'd checked her eyes for any signs. He was accustomed to working with individuals using drugs and felt she did not appear to be high on drugs. Lovingly, but firmly, he sent her away.

I never saw her again.

My daughter, who also had her hair done at the girl's shop, called the next week for an appointment. The operator reported that the number had been disconnected. My daughter drove over to the shop. It was deserted. I also drove by. No salon! At that time, I should have contacted the strip-mall manager to see what had happened to the family and why the salon was closed. My friend who'd been going there for several years had planned to follow up for me. We did nothing. All of us were unwilling to consider the possibilities of what may have happened.

I certainly felt strange and even guilty. Was this my doing or lack thereof? What could I have done? I hadn't really believed her. Do I now? I just don't know.

My friend, her client, also had thought the poor girl had been losing her marbles for the two weeks we were involved. She encouraged me to steer clear of her. I think of her still. Nothing was ever in the papers. Where is this girl? Where is her whole family?

UFO Experience

I had another UFO experience during the same time period, but earlier than the "deep cleft in my arm" experience. I awoke one night to find myself sitting upright in my bed in the darkness. I was frightened, shaking in a cold room, my mind full of what I was remembering as having just happened. Here is the excerpt from my journal of that day.

"It was not a dream. I have just been visited by three non-human strangers. They did not terrify me when I saw them in my bedroom. It is difficult to describe them as they had indistinct faces atop very tall forms. They were shadowy and I just knew they were not of this world. They seemed friendly. They showed me some meat they'd brought along from wherever they came from. I told them I was a vegetarian. It didn't seem to get through to them. The meat was in square, plastic type-boxes. They told me that before the boxes were sealed, the air around the meat was sprayed with a substance that preserved it indefinitely without any change to its texture or taste. They insisted I touch the packages. They were soft to my touch. How convenient that would be to a person coming home hungry and not wanting to wait for meat to thaw. They also said that it could be stored outside of a freezer, in a pantry.

They all wanted to feel my hair because I was in need of a touch-up and my brown roots were showing next to my scalp on my bleached blond head. They wanted to know if the color of my hair was in the process of changing its color and why. They had never heard of hair-color products. They giggled like small children. I tried that morning to recall their voices, but realized I never had heard them. I just knew in my mind what they were saying.

There was more, but I was not able to put it into words. I'm still excited by this visit and very in awe of them. They told me philosophies that were similar to our vegetarian beliefs and said they did not eat meat. Then why the meat? It was definitely a part of their diet, their protein, but they couldn't understand my question about the meat. What was in those preserved packages?

We mystics view all Creation as one divine manifestation. So these visitors, too, are a part of us, important in the divine plan. We are not alone.

Have we been learning from them since ancient Atlantis or is it that they are learning from us? Are they in a parallel universe? Was this perhaps in an exchange of knowledge? They seemed infinitely wiser than we are and others have speculated that they have the ability to circumnavigate the universe at incredible speeds. We know so very little about others (extraterrestrials) that may inhabit the larger universe.

We have been unable to convert matter into energy, but just during my lifetime we've learned to break the sound barrier and the heat barrier, and visit other planets. What wonders await my great-grandchildren? Surely someday we'll be able to explain the visitors, learn from them and share with them, to everyone's benefit. Some reports make them seem very friendly, others are ominous. Just like our own people would be if they ventured into their world. I wish I could hang around to enjoy what may someday become ordinary. I do plan to be here for a little while longer and I will keep an open mind.

Chapter 11

Out of Body Experience (OOBE) and Other Oddities

I want to tell you about Astral Travel or Out of Body Experience (OOBE). Because of all my unusual experiences, the personal knowledge I gained while having an Out-of-Body Experience has changed my fear of death. I believe that when the time comes, I can embrace death as described in William Cullen Bryant's great poem "Thanatopsis." Bryant writes, "By an unfaltering trust, approach thy grave, / Like one who wraps the drapery of his couch / About him, and lies down to pleasant dreams." (80-81).

It is natural to age, but I plan to have a perfect death experience, by choice not by chance. It is possible to leave one's body without illness or pain. I do not plan on using them as an excuse. I will be productive, healthy and active until I go into my non-physical body. I am not afraid.

Being Out of One's Body

Astral Travel is when a person's astral-self detaches from one's body and moves about, fully conscious and supernaturally mobile. It is believed that man is made up of two components: the first being a soul or spirit, God, in and as us; and the second, a material body of flesh and blood for us to use while we are on the Earth plane. As well, it is thought by many that each of us has a third form, an astral body – literally, "starry body" – a body of light, an exact copy of our flesh and blood body. And, wonder of wonders, it is capable of separating itself from our physical body! Many people claim to have seen this shiny, luminous material leave the body at death. This astral body survives death, can pass through ceilings, walls and other solid obstructions. It is connected to us by a cord, described as silver.

There are many books devoted to this subject alone, books that teach one how to have the wonderful experience of being out of one's body. I'd read a handful, borrowed from the library or purchased for my library, but my first episode was unplanned and awesome.

I was at the dentist, in the chair and he was having trouble filling a back molar because I kept gagging. I was trying not to gag, but having no success. He was ready to give up so I went to my

Alpha level to see if I could relax enough for him to proceed. Suddenly I felt myself leave my body and I was floating upwards. I knew just enough to know what was happening and I was enraptured. There was such a feeling of weightlessness. It was like one feels in a swimming pool, a buoyancy. I found myself suspended in the ceiling and over in a corner of the room watching the dentist work on my mouth. I realized from my reading on the subject that this was an O.B.E. How utterly fascinating to see one's own physical body from that angle, and in that state. It was summer and I was wearing open-toed sandals. I felt a flush of embarrassment to see that my toenail polish was chipped.

The next thing I knew the dentist was shaking my arm, saying, "June, are you all right?" He was amazed that I had gotten control of my gag reflex. He said I'd been so motionless that he'd been able to get all the work done without pause and he complimented me on my self-control. I just told him I'd used self-hypnosis – not a real lie. No need for him to have had proof that he was working on a kook.

This phenomenon, my introduction into 'life-after-life', left me with the great benefaction of KNOWING I will survive physical death. Most of us humans greatly fear death, a fear of the unknown, a fear generated by our church's teaching of a Hell-fire we believe we probably deserve. I am FEARLESS. What a gift!

Out of Body Experience

On another occasion, I was in a bar with my good friend, John, from my day job whom I dated briefly. The bar was across from John's apartment, a place where 'everybody knew our names.' The cute, young cocktail waitress who called us by name and even introduced us to any interesting newcomers was our server that evening. She was aware of my otherworldly skills and asked for my help. Her boyfriend was in New Orleans for a new job and they'd agreed to have a trial separation, no phone calls, and no letters. They'd been talking of marriage, but had some problems. I'd never met him, but the tears in her eyes moved me. It had only been one week since he'd left and she wondered if I could send him a mental telepathy message that she loved him and wished he'd break his promise and call her. I assured her I'd make an attempt when I reached home to the quiet of my bedroom.

I had no clue as to where he was in New Orleans or what he looked like. In the Mind Control class we'd been instructed to create a laboratory workshop in our imagination, a place for us to do our psychic work. Mine was on a rocky cliff at the ocean's edge. It was a contemporary rock house jutting out over the cliff. In the lab I had a comfortable, soft leather recliner beside a file cabinet full of resource material on everything that had ever happened in the world since the beginning of time and into the future till the end, including material on names and places of everyone.

Yes, our imaginations are this encompassing – we just find it difficult to access. Hence the Mind Control idea of believing one has a place to go seek answers for a challenge. I found this so captivating. In my lab, on the other side to the left of my recliner I'd created a huge, stone fireplace. Beside it was a complete lab with test tubes and bottles, a la Frankenstein. All this I could bring into my awareness by putting three fingers together on each hand. Then all I had to do was ask myself a question, mentally look up the answers in my files or work in my lab.

I've never ceased to marvel at how magnificent our minds are if we just ask for access to the knowledge stored there. Nowadays, I'm sure that in the Mind Control classes they've added the use of computers, but I'm still using my antiquated files and lab that I learned in 1970. The mind is our greatest tool, greater than any computer ever created. Our minds are God's mind for our personal use!

So I employed this technique to find the cocktail waitress's boyfriend in another city. To my total amazement I was, for the second time, out of my body and in my ceiling. Next I was hovering over his bed in New Orleans. I knew I was there by the feeling and the sight of the iron bedstead and the plantation shutters. He was asleep, a handsome, blond fellow who looked to be very tall. His feet hung over the foot of the bed because he was longer than the mattress. I just KNEW this was her boyfriend. I leaned down and whispered into his ear that his girlfriend loved him, missed him and wished he would call. He didn't stir. I didn't seem to have disturbed his sleep.

It was very late and I felt extremely tired. I still felt frisky though in my buoyancy. He might not remember my message when he awakened, but I was in the crescent city that I loved, and instantly I found myself in the Quarter floating above Bourbon Street. Even at this midnight hour lights were blazing and the streets were crowded with tourists. I've enjoyed the French Quarter many times since as my son has a home there, but never again from on high. Well, I've been 'high' there, but only on daiquiris. I've never told my son about my midnight solo tour.

Two nights later we were back in the bar. The waitress rushed to our table with the news that the following morning after seeing me last she'd heard from her boyfriend. He'd said, "Something just told me you'd welcome a call from me."

She said I must have contacted him. I told her I'd done better than that, that I'd whispered it in his ear. I asked her if he was unusually tall, as I'd noticed his feet hung off the foot of the bed. At first she was dumb struck, then she insisted that I'd met him or someone in the bar had told me he was over six feet. John assured her I had not met or heard of him except when she'd asked for help.

She tried to pay me. I told her I'd had too much fun being out of my body. She must have believed I was bonkers, but she bought us each a drink.

Another OOBE

The third time I had an OOBE, I was visiting my mother in San Antonio. I was upset over a boyfriend I'll tell you about in the next chapter. He was a past-life soul mate, now returned to me. Lying in bed in the guest room at my mom's, almost crying, I found myself, once again, in the ceiling with the wonderful feeling of weightlessness, hovering like a helicopter over my physical body in the bed. As I looked down on myself, my face slowly changed into his face, superimposed over mine. I shuddered and was instantly back in my body.

I had to tell someone, as I was worried about what I'd seen. I told my friend Suzette when I was back home in Dallas. She interpreted that the vision I'd had of my face changing was a very serious omen of trouble coming. She said this intense love affair was headed for some very dark days with no satisfactory ending. Boy, was she ever right.

Other Oddities

I woke up one morning with the word 'mem' on my mind. What could it mean? I thought it must be short for 'memory' and wondered what I was supposed to remember. I felt strongly that it was important. When I could not come up with anything in meditation I got up and looked in my large dictionary. Mem is the thirteenth letter in the Hebrew alphabet and means 'water'– still a puzzle.

I dressed and went into my kitchen. When I looked out the patio French doors I saw my swimming pool full of roofing shingles. I was having a new roof installed and the roofers, leaving for the weekend, had left bundles of asbestos shingles on the sloping area where they were working. There had been terrible wind and rain that night and now the shingles were in my pool. I called the roofer, even though it was Sunday, and he got right to work calling his men. He knew it would ruin all the water in the pool and if left longer could even damage the bottom of the pool's surface.

MeM? Was someone from the other side trying to get my attention? In Hebrew? Could it have been my deceased father, a Danish Jew? Or was it even Jesus himself, though Jesus spoke Aramaic, or was it Greek? I find metaphysics a joy, a hobby more exciting than prospecting for gold, which my Husband Sam and I tried on our honeymoon in Alaska.

When a dream awakens us it is always an important message. One night I sat up in bed suddenly. I was remembering that I'd just been in conversation with an old friend, an artist who had died several years earlier. He told me that I needed to call our mutual friend, David, another artist, who was having a birthday 'on the morrow.' We had talked about the fact that David was bi-polar and became unbalanced when not taking his meds, but was always a sweet, likable fellow. I promised to pass along the message that he was remembered and wished a happy birthday form the other side.

I made a mental note to check the next morning to see if it was truly David's birthday. I knew I could check by looking under David's name in my appointment book because I'd read for him and I always made a note of my client's birth dates.

Should I have been surprised? Of course it was his birthday. So I called him. He was touched. David is that friend we all have who seems the neediest and runs along the precarious border between sanity and madness. How great a love there was between these two artists that from beyond the grave one would show concern for the other. This was proof for me that it is very important to surround our departed loved ones with the light of the Christ-consciousness. Where there is light there is no darkness.

Articles in an Old Home

A fellow salesman at the furniture store where I worked bought a wonderful, hundred year old house. He was restoring it at night and on his days off. He was faithfully following guidelines from the local Historical Society. He asked me if I'd meditate on the house and see if there were any jewels or money hidden in the walls. Seemed like a fun project to me.

The next day I reported to him that there were no valuables to find but there was something he needed in the wall behind the washing machine. He told me that wall was new and he'd just finished installing the washer the night before, but with his faith in me, he pulled out the washer and the wall, and there behind the new sheetrock was the hammer he'd been searching for everywhere. I love being psychic when it's that much fun.

When I married and moved to the Texas Hill Country, my husband had an English Shepherd. I'd been so fortunate that my fear of large dogs had been resolved by a regression session I'd undergone (Chapter Twelve). I'd avoided all dogs all my life, but now I had learned to love this one. He was very lonely because our other dog had died. We decided we needed to adopt a buddy for him.

During this search for a dog we visited friends in Tyler, Texas. I fell in love with their dog. I learned that he was a Norwegian Elkhound. That night, while meditating, I programmed my mind that I would soon find a dog of that breed. When we got back home there was a message from a friend that she'd found a dog for us. She said it was a mixed-breed of Husky and German Shepherd. She convinced us we should at least meet this dog. Her owners were moving and could not take her. For my husband it was love at first sight.

We called our vet the next day and took her in for a check over. On the vet's patient sheet under breed we wrote, "Husky and German Shepherd." He took one look at her and said, "This is not a Husky or a German Shepherd. This is a Norwegian Elkhound." Be careful what you ask for, spirit will deliver in kind. I was jubilant, my husband incredulous. He was still learning what it meant to be married to this unearthly lady.

Conversation with a Scorpion

The Hill Country is home to scorpions by the millions as the soil is mostly limestone rocks. Very soon I was bitten on the shoulder by one who'd hidden himself in my nightgown – must have been a male. It was a very painful experience. I wasn't looking forward to a life shared with these sometimes deadly insects. The Bible gives us dominion over all God's creatures and I felt I should be able to live in harmony with them if I could just figure out a way. I, once more, went to my Alpha level and was guided to ask to speak with the head scorpion. I didn't feel foolish at the time. It was a dreadful experience, squeamish as I am. All around me I felt a dark, maroon denseness with a monstrous 'something' I took to be whom I needed to speak to. I made it an offer (blackmail, if you will) – I'd kill no scorpions outside my house, ever, if he would keep his creatures out of my dwelling.

My husband joined me in this promise. If we moved an old board or a rock outside and saw a scorpion, we left it alone. In nineteen years of living there, we were never again bothered with seeing them in the house. Neighbors would note that the year had been especially bad with these many-legged horrors and I'd smile smugly and say I hadn't noticed. I sure didn't tell the neighbors. They all continued to shake out their shoes in the morning, the common cautionary measure in the Hill Country.

My Dog, My Protector

After my divorce, when I was again single and involved with Mind Control classes, I came home from work one night, got ready for bed and sat down to meditate. I went into my imaginary laboratory and lying there on a rug in front of the large, stone fireplace was a huge German Shepherd. I was startled.

"Who are you?" I asked, never expecting an answer.

"I'm here for your protection", the dog said, not in an actual voice, but in my mind.

"I don't need protection."

"Yes you do! You forgot to lock your doors!"

I jumped up and sure enough my glass sliding doors were unlocked. The angel-dog stayed by the hearth for years. I always saw him there until I married my second husband and moved away from Dallas.

Protection from Above

After both of my parents had died I was left with their house in San Antonio in an area that had developed through the years into being a primarily Hispanic neighborhood. My mom and step dad had a troublesome neighbor who had stolen things from their yard, tools and even lawn furniture. I lived thirty minutes out in the Hill Country to the north and was concerned that he would take advantage of no one being there, taking the opportunity to break in and rob the house.

I came up with the idea of telling the neighborhood gossip-woman that I was a Bruja, a Mexican witch, and could put a spell on people. For three months the house remained unoccupied and was never vandalized. Even the yard furniture stayed in place. It was a small, non-violent, close to the truth, lie on my part, but it worked.

Chapter 12

Reincarnation

What advantage can be found in having a life reading? It is a reading that concentrates on a former lifetime of ours. In many cases it has been a great help in understanding problems of this lifetime, and adding an extra dimension to my existence. Among a majority of the world's population the theories of re-birth, karmic debt, and the supra-physical body are accepted or are at least being seriously studied.

Reincarnation, a concept of an undying soul, it is said was universally accepted by the early Christians. However, as it challenges the traditional western concepts of life and death, it fell into disfavor for emphasizing the physical over our spiritual eternal life. There are many accounts theorizing how reincarnation may have been removed from the early Bible and controversy continues even today. It has been surmised that it was the Early Church that succeeded in having reincarnation removed from our present Bible and that there are still traces remaining that seemingly were missed by the elders.

Until I had first-hand experience I felt dubious about psychics who dealt with reincarnation. I felt that they could tell one anything and what proof would there be? It really comes down to belief in their honesty and their ability. For me it has been a case of does the information presented to me ring a bell? Is this information dredged up from the collective consciousness? Couldn't it apply to any of us? So how does one judge for one's self except by ringing that bell?

It rang for me, for the first time, when I personally experienced a former lifetime that applied to a current problem. Among many other books that I read, I had been introduced to past-life readings by Dr. Gina Cerminara's book, *Many Mansions* in which she writes about the Edgar Cayce Story on reincarnation. Cayce is called the Sleeping Prophet, and was a Christian man who believed in reincarnation. I also read all of Joan Grant's books written from her memories of past lives, and Jan Price's *The Other Side of Death*. I was especially intrigued with this subject since my friend Suzy had scared me with the idea that I might have to be married to the same abusive man again in a future incarnation.

So, I was attending a seminar in Dallas when the main speaker announced that he would hold a demonstration on regression – going back to a past life – and, unexpectedly, asked me if I would be his aide. I felt able to respond. It seemed important to me to be a part of a demonstration of regression. I thought it would be easy for me. He knew me and knew I had had two wisdom teeth extracted from my jawbone with only hypnosis and no pain medication. Hypnosis generally takes a few minutes before the hypnotist can proceed with instructions for the subject. He had not wanted to ask me ahead of time for fear the audience would think we had rehearsed and he knew I would go 'under' very quickly.

He seated me in a chair facing the audience and suggested that I close my eyes. Then he told me to relax and to mentally go up into the sky above the city. I vividly remember seeing all of Dallas spread out beneath me with its millions of lights. It was exhilarating. I was aware of being inside the building AND in the sky. Ordinarily I have a fear of heights so this was surprising and fascinating for me.

Please don't ever pass up the chance to experience a past lifetime through hypnosis. It was mind-boggling. I knew, at all times, that I was in Dallas, Texas, but was visiting another century.

It was a thrill akin to skydiving and made me proud to have dared this first-hand experience. I must add a warning, though; it is a force of the mind that is too powerful to be a parlor game. It must be undertaken only by an experienced hypnotist.

Then the regressionist proposed I come down to earth in another lifetime. He told me to tell him when I felt myself on solid ground.

When I said that I was standing on soft, leaf-covered earth in a forest of huge trees, he started his questions. He asked me to look down at my feet and tell him what kind of shoes I was wearing. I was surprised to find my feet wrapped in rags. The audience laughed. This, too, I was conscious of as being a reality.

He said, "Are you carrying anything?"

"Faggots", I answered. Again the audience laughed.

He admonished them not to laugh as it might be distracting and explained that a faggot was also a term for sticks of wood.

I had been one of the Forest People, living alone in a heavily wooded area belonging to an Earl who lived in a castle on the estate. We determined I was in England. The faggots were for an open fire pit where I cooked my 'potions' outside a crude hut that was my dwelling. I made a meager living selling charms, cures and herbs. I cast spells and read tarot cards. We talked about those things for a while and then he took me forward in time to ask about how I had died. I said that I had sold the Earl's wife a powder to put in the Earl's mead (a drink) to make him impotent. She had hated having sex with him as he was brutal and he stank. He found out what I had done for her and together with his several huge mastiff doges, he hunted me down in the forest and set the dogs on me. Their jaws were on my throat.

He brought me back to full consciousness when I started moaning and crying out. I was shaken but I related to the audience all that had happened to me in those last moments of that life. I answered many questions from the assembly. I received an enthusiastic hand and many even stood up to clap but I was in a state of shock because I realized why I had had a life-long need to flee away from large dogs. It is true that if one can relive a death experience it can cure one from any left-over trauma caused by that death. It did this for me and my fear of large dogs.

Consciously, I knew nothing at that time about Mastiffs, couldn't have even described one, but to this day I can shut my eyes and vividly recall what I experienced that night. Those huge, open, slobbering jaws, sharp teeth and my blood spurting out gave me no pain that night but a sense of dreadful terror. Reliving one's death under hypnosis is not painful but can be very traumatic.

Only years later did I see, up close and personal, a real Mastiff. My husband and I were on an outing at Lost Maples Park in Texas. On the path under the Maple trees we met a man with a large dog on a leash. A sudden chill shot down my spine. I stared in the dog's face. He was panting, with saliva dripping in long, white strings from his large jaws.

I asked, "What kind of dog is he?"

The man stopped and said, "He's a Mastiff."

"Do they ordinarily drool?"

"Yes."

I shuddered, remembering their drool as they bit and tore at my flesh, but I was not afraid to touch this dog, and did! The trauma was gone from my soul.

This further convinced me that I had actually experienced a genuine past life. It also proved to me the great benefits as I soon married Sam, a man who had two German Shepherds. I might have passed on his proposal if it had come a few years earlier. How sad that would have been.

I was able, also, to now explain my unusually strong interest in herbs. I've explored the curative powers of herbs, never realizing I was renewing an ancient skill, one cut short by intense cruelty. I had only wanted to help that poor

woman with my herbs. I'd paid a monstrous price
– my life.

Thirty Years Ago . .

I saw him 'across a crowded room.' Yes, it
happens and it is always a friend from a former
lifetime, usually because of important, unfinished
business. Are you still with me, reader? Then here
is my biggest secret, and one of which I am not
proud. "Peter" was an artist with incredible talent.
We each taught an art class at a picture framer's
art gallery. I first saw him across a group of easels,
among his adult students who were bending
earnestly over fresh canvases. It was a head-on-
collision for both of us.

Our eyes met and I felt like my hair had
been set on fire! I batted my mascara-laden-lashes
at him and was rewarded with a huge grin. As I
look off into the distance today, I can still bring to
my mind a clear image of him. A man in his forties,
he was not really handsome, though later I thought
that he was. He had reddish brown hair and lots of
it, in the style of the seventies. That longer cut was
invented just for him. I had always favored dark-
headed, testosterone-strong men in dark Italian-
cut suits with dress shirts and conservative ties. He
wore blue jeans – they did have a sharp crease – an
open-collared white dress shirt, tucked in. In Texas
that is the look favored by our Cowboys in town for
a good time on Saturday night.

He could have been ANY type and I would still have fallen into the sky over his brown eyes. You talk about drowning in someone's eyes – I was upside down – I could have floated all the way UP to paradise.

I could have looked at his perfect face for hours. When we sat across from one another in restaurants I would look at him and break into delighted laughter. I loved holding his face in my hands and just memorizing his features while smiling at the joy of having found him. I couldn't believe my good luck! There was this feeling for both of us that we'd found what had been lost. When we kissed it was like we'd just shrugged off the world and we were alone together even in a crowd.

He was tall and tanned with a flat stomach from years of carrying the U.S. mail in a large, quiet, tree-lined neighborhood. He had taken that civil service job because it paid expenses and left him free from midday till bedtime to paint. He drove a late model Cadillac and wore a Timex watch. When I called that an oxymoron, he said, "No, no, I like a Timex because it's so dependable, so is my Cadillac." So from the beginning I began to endow him with qualities I later learned he did not possess.

We were both married, both unhappy. I'd already left my husband twice only to return with my tail between my legs because I could not find a good-paying job. We were together every free moment. I did not realize it then but we were renewing ancient bonds.

Our art classes now had two teachers because we were a pair and our lucky students benefited. Our teaching methods coincided perfectly. We even took our combined classes on Saturday field trips to paint in the outdoors where we'd located old barns and picturesque brooks. He impressed me with picking up discarded cans and trash, complaining about people messing up the landscape. He was so sensitive to our environment. How endearing!

Of course there's something so dreadfully wrong about a love affair that starts with a divorce, something against the laws of the Universe. But we were sincere and talked marriage from our first day and agreed that he would go first with leaving his wife. After only a week from our initial eye contact he moved out of the house he shared with his wife, into a small apartment, and filed for a divorce. He gave his wife everything, even his beloved Caddy, and bought himself a Volkswagen camper.

Peter said he loved me so much he promised to always clean my art brushes for me and in his turpentine. Hey, you artists, is that real love or what?

My divorce, several months later, was the best thing I ever did. As you've read, it freed me to be a professional psychic and gave me the self-confidence that I could take care of myself. I sold furniture and gave readings, he delivered mail and painted; we were delirious. We floated! Our feet never touched the ground. Life was a twenty-four/seven passionate dream. When he would walk in my door, we would head for my sturdiest table where the Postman always rang twice.

We had pet names for ourselves. I called him "Number 9." Our largest brushes were number nines. Figure that out! Every day he wrote passionate love letters to me even though we were together. He signed them "9". I still have them all, yellowing in a pretty box on my dresser.

I was holding off on setting a date. Marriage frightened me. All went well until I became aware of his possessiveness. I couldn't even join a girlfriend for a movie without inciting his jealous, temper outburst. What was happening here in my personal paradise? This was beyond a lover's desire for being together. He would not share my time with my grown and married kids. I could have understood some of the mistrust. Jealousy can even be complimentary in small doses. I, too, was usually unwilling to share our time together, but adding even one other person to our mix made it uncomfortable. I was being stifled with this over-the-top rage. He had me concerned about our future. But, being a person who desires peace-at-any-price, I tried to ignore the warnings. Every once-in-a-blue something comes along that scrambles our preconceptions and makes us a whole different omelet. I now had these changes to deal with.

Since I'd had twenty-nine years of experience with a controlling husband I recognized the signs and it made me cautious. I wanted no more of that problem and so we argued a great deal; me with my wonderful, new found independence, him with his sullen brooding. He wanted to marry. It became all he talked about. It was too soon for me. I was still reeling. I should have been warned to keep my seatbelt fastened and my tray table in the full and upright and locked position!

Peter called me at work on Valentine's Day that first year. "I have a Valentine gift for you," he said, "I just married my ex-wife since you didn't want to marry me. Goodbye!"

I was devastated. I just couldn't wrap my brain around it. Marry an ex? Isn't that going backwards? I mourned for him as through he had died. The song was gone from my heart. I couldn't work. I was drowning in a sea of pain. All I wanted was for the pain to stop. Every day I awoke on the dark side of dawn. I had been eaten empty by his consuming love. I felt like a shell whose sea-creature had abandoned it and left it to wash up, empty, on a lonely beach. I lay burning in the sand but could not feel the heat, only a cold emptiness.

I was so bewildered by his crazy solution to our problem. I was in agony. I wanted the world to stop so I could get off and go to a better world. Perhaps Venus, known for love. Even today, these many years later I cannot write this story without tears in my eyes. Tears exorcise emotions that will otherwise haunt and embitter us. I'm glad I cried hours on end back then for I did find freedom and I had not left the world.

I'd been doing research for my psychic readings by going to every psychic I could locate, sometimes driving to other cities. Most of them, I found, asked too many questions and seemed to be reading only from hints I felt I had inadvertently passed to them in answer to their questions. But, I'd uncovered an excellent regressionist. She also became a dear friend, but at this time she knew nothing of my problems. I realized Peter had to be a Karmic problem and I hoped to learn what I had done to him in a past life that could have caused this abrupt ending of our romance. I did not reveal anything about Peter. Please suspend disbelief for this next paragraph.

This regressionist took me way, way back to Atlantis, that legendary land that is believed to have sunk beneath the sea during one of Earth's great geological upheavals. It is consensually agreed that the inhabitants of Atlantis were far ahead of our present time in their technology. We found that in my past lifetime there I had been married to Peter. We were scientists working together in the field of ophthalmology. Our experiments included transplanting animal eyes into humans and human eyes into animals – for what purpose is still unclear to me. These experiments were done without the consent of those directly involved. They seemed to be slaves or prisoners. We disagreed about what we were doing. I thought it was inhumane and I was opposed to further studies. Finally, I fled from the lab and from him. For the rest of his life he had looked endlessly for me and had never found me. I'd had help from what would now be a "witness protection and relocation program."

My regressionist took me to other lifetimes with Peter. One in particular was in Denmark. My father, in this incarnation, migrated from Denmark. But back then, again as Peter's wife, we lived on a large estate and I had left him once more, this time to run off with our butcher, the man in charge of butchering and preparing all the meats. This butcher was the same man I was married to for twenty-nine years in this life.

Strange how that rang the bell of truth for me. My ex in this life was well known in Dallas as 'Smoky Jack,' the barbeque king; a popular caterer.

So, back to Peter. Whenever we've been together in the many lifetimes in the past, I've always left him. He had a strong subconscious fear of losing me that he did not understand, and I reinforced his fears with my reluctance to marry him. I left the session with a great deal of understanding about my lover.

There are loves with too much fire and pain to be long lasting. They burn themselves to ash. Such was the love I found with Peter. Can you understand how important a role reincarnation can play in our lives?

Peter was back with his wife, but our story does not end here. In only one week he was on the phone with me begging for forgiveness, pleading to see me. I loved him, so I found myself in the disgusting position of dating a married man. Do our hearts betray us? When I finally tried to break it off, once again he obtained a divorce. What was it with this man? I could write some heart-wrenching country western lyrics.

Then, again, the nagging and temper outbursts started. I threw him out of my house (almost physically). After a month of silence, I called his apartment – after all I was still enamored – his line had been disconnected. I called him at the Gallery. The owner told me he'd gotten married! I assumed he was back with his wife. Wrong! He'd met someone new, a widow with money and a large house.

I heard from him within a month. He came, crying, and fell into my arms. He was sorry. He LOVED me. This time I didn't tell myself that undoubtedly he loved me, and when he declared he'd get a divorce if I'd promise to marry him I almost laughed. Was he demented? I could not make that promise. By now the idea of marriage to him was too frightening to discuss. Then, there were, again, many ugly, angry words between us.

He was a man-on-a-mission, hell-bent on divorce. During a particularly nasty confrontation with his poor unsuspecting new wife, he blurted out his love for me and she ran from her house. It was morning during a pouring spring rain and she was driving very fast. She drove headlong into a telephone pole at sixty miles an hour and was instantly killed.

The police could not locate him. After contacting the gallery owner they came to the furniture store to talk with me. I did have a call from him earlier, but could not be of any help as to his whereabouts.

His poor wife had the misfortune of meeting him in the midst of this violent love affair with me. What chance had there been for her happiness? Of course she'd married him before giving herself time to get to know him. She'd paid for that mistake with her life.

His existence was drastically altered at that point. He'd inherited her house and a great deal of money even though the marriage was of so short a duration. She had no relatives, no children to object. With this windfall he retired from the post office. He painted full time. He opened his own gallery. He even seemed happy. He started to drink, not his usual one or two beers, but strong bourbon. He'd never done that before. His personality changed, and not for the better.

The day he gained the inheritance he asked me to marry him or at least move into HER house with him. Oh, what fresh hell was that for me? He got another fast rejection. This was not just a hell of a romance, it was a romance 'gone to hell.' I was finished! DONE! Stick a fork in me. I was no longer besotted!

I spoke with him often, almost tongue-in-cheek now. He'd married again, another poor, foolish woman he'd known for only two weeks. I'd suggested a psychologist for him to get his thoughts straightened out. His new wife had been the receptionist! Peter met with this psychologist only one time, but managed to steal his "girl Friday."

At this point with me he'd turned into a cartoon character. What was he all about? Was this a (fantasy) Walt Disney World? Was he Mickey Mouse or Goofy? Am I Bippidi-Boppidi-Boo?

Four months later – longer this time – he had filed once again. I suggested he call another psychologist, not to save his marriage, but to save his life. He needed to see someone who would have the professional skills to recognize that he had a serious emotional or physical problem. Are you still with me on this emotional roller coaster?

Then you've guessed it – he married again – to a nurse this time.

This was marriage number five, in case you have lost count. He must have had that Liz Taylor quality. He HAD to marry his conquests. He HAD to make honest women out of them. He could not ravish and run. I believe it came from his centuries old feeling that his love would soon leave him.

This time I felt he had accidentally chosen wisely, a nurse for his problems. It still hurts me somewhat. There was still a bit of that 'ole-feelin', but I was now involved with someone less explosive and I was very into my readings. I saw Peter on a limited basis. He had bought a camper. He wanted me to go camping with him near Luckenbach, Texas, where 'Willie and Waylon and the boys' hung out. We both loved to paint the huge Spanish oaks and the lush cedars that grew along the Guadalupe River in the Hill Country. His marriage was a joke at this point and I needed to visit my mom in near San Antonio. So ignoring the fact that he had a wife, I consented to a long weekend vacation.

I followed him down, driving my own car. It was a miserable five to six hour trip. His driving was so erratic. He would speed for a time, going over the limit and then abruptly slow down to forty. Once I passed and hailed him to a stop and told him I was about to open a can of ass-whippin' if he didn't maintain a constant speed and get us there before dark. He was drinking beer, but did not appear to be intoxicated and laughed at my temper tantrum. So we resumed our driving and his was less aberrant.

When we got settled for the night at a KOA camp just five miles from Luckenbach, I finally told him about my visit to the regressionist. I had felt guilty keeping that information from him about possibly why we had had so much trouble on the subject of marriage. I felt guilty, also, that I had always rejected him. It was his disregard for all things metaphysical that had held me back from sharing the reading of our life in Atlantis. He had always been difficult enough without my adding any fuel to his fire. I was more interested in getting him into my bed. Surprisingly, with this news, he seemed to be at least interested. And then, a shocker, he asked me why I'd never read for him. "You've read for all my friends, but never me," he complained.

"You've never believed in me," I answered. So I read for him that first day of what was to be our weekend-long vacation. I always took my geode with me wherever I traveled. It had its own little navy blue and gold Cutty Sark sack with the gold cord tie. I lit a candle. Womanizers always have candles, so, of course, his camper had them. I laid down on his bed with my rock on my stomach and counted myself down and said my prayers.

I was horrified to see, almost immediately, a large, brain tumor in his skull. I sat up with tears streaming down my face and told him what I'd just seen. He cried too. He believed me. He said that explained the severe headaches he'd been having. It also explained a hell of a lot to me about his enormous defects of character.

I tried to get him to wait till the next day, but he left immediately, back for Dallas. I drove south to San Antonio and my mother's.

When I got back to Dallas two days later I made one of my rare phone calls to him. He answered the phone. His nurse-wife had gotten him into a doctor right away. He did indeed have a brain tumor. The x-rays showed a tumor, too large to be removed, with tentacles that wrapped around the back of the eyes. The doctor told him he was going blind. They also told his wife that he would probably soon become violent and she must be prepared to call them and they would come with restraints and take him away.

She left him the next day. After all he was almost a stranger to her. In some kind of defense of her actions I reminded him of the short time he had known her.

The final time I saw Peter was because he called me to come to his house to take any of his paintings I might want to remember him by. Mercy, remember him? I would carry him in my heart all the rest of the days of my life.

I took no paintings. I already had many of his works and still do. I went because I did want to see him one last time. His first wife, the mother of his children, was coming the next day to move him back home with her.

He was completely blind now. His eyes will always haunt me. They were a bright cobalt blue, shiny, with no depth. I was nauseated. I wanted to run out the door. I did not want to touch him. I did manage to stay for a respectable length of time. I turned down his further offer of a painting.

I drove home crying so hard it was difficult to see. It was raining. The whole world seemed to be crying with me for this talented artist, now lost. Our gallery owner told me he had lived another two months. I had no place at his funeral and did not attend. I'd already said my goodbyes.

Reminiscence

If I had been unconvinced of reincarnation before, I was certainly a believer now. And Karma? What more evidence of Karma does one need than this, that a man who had unfeelingly taken the eyes of living people and transplanted then into animals should himself lose the sight in his own eyes? For an artist this is the most dreadful fate of all. His Karma had waited until this lifetime, when his artist-eyes were his everything, to collect its age-old debt.

My own eyesight, five years later, was almost taken away in my left eye. My debt would have been less, remember, because I had chosen to leave that lab in Atlantis. So I was spared.

I've done a great deal of research that gives me the assurance that we do not have to pay Karmic debt in this lifetime if we "seek ye first the Kingdom," meaning get in touch with our Kingdom within, our higher self, our God presence. Meditation is our passageway to oneness with the Father. So, I was granted the priceless privilege of regaining my sight. Thank you, Father.

My beloved Peter, artist, friend and lover, has come to me many times in dreams and we will meet again but never again in that intense collision of matching souls. I don't believe it happens often. I reject it ever happening to me again. No longer do I plan to be his lover in a future life; perhaps a close, loving relative, a loving brother or sister, maybe! I believe we have made our peace and he, at last, is at peace.

Has reincarnation been proven? Believing that each soul has but one lifetime on earth is like believing that each house has but one room. I believe that the house of my soul is a mansion with many, many glorious rooms. To those who believe, it is an irrefutable fact; to skeptics, it is an interesting coincidence and just plain fiction. I have found that searching within has been my evidence.

Chapter 13

About Psychics – No Secrets Held Back

Today most psychics get no respect. Much of the blame for that must rest with us because of the many lunatics and scam artists. I don't believe many of us plan to be charlatans. It is just an easy out when one yearns to be better at this elusive craft. The old tricks of the gypsy fortunetellers are still widespread. Silver crossing their palms is always their goal, and lying becomes second nature to them. How can one tell when encountering these fakes? It's difficult because they do have psychic talents and tell us just enough truths to enthrall us, and then, wham, they report that we are in great danger from an enemy out to harm us. They then offer to burn candles to protect us; candles are dearly priced and foolishly useless except in the hands of true psychics who usually use them for protection. The time it happened to me I stood up, thanked the reader, paid the original fee agreed upon and left. That was a long time ago and at that time she wanted twenty-five dollars each for four candles. I had no enemies and even if, what nonsense that was?

Gypsies Perhaps

Gypsies, as a religious group, are trained from birth to be opportunists. They work on developing their third eye and some are true psychics. But embellishing half-truths and telling outright untruths are opportunities that their religion does not shy away from when opportunity presents itself. Given an inch, you might expect a trained opportunist to take a mile.

Many readers start by asking questions. It's easy for a person to blurt out the problems they have questions about; the gypsy fortune tellers seem very talented when they rephrase your problem and give back to you what you have just told them. Solutions from an outsider's view point are not very difficult. Psychic powers are unnecessary to a person who is naturally good at solving life's problems. They read one's facial expressions and tell us what they think we want to hear. Readings are magical, not magic.

It is wise to bring one's own tape recorder and two fresh tapes. If the soothsayer would not permit me to tape the reading, I would become suspicious and usually leave.

The Merriam-Webster Dictionary definition of soothsayer: a person who predicts the future by magical, intuitive, or more rational means : prognosticator. ttp://www.merriam webster.com.

Why wouldn't they want us to have a record of what they said? Do they think we will sue? Oh yes, I can see the scene in court and my lawyer saying, "Your Honor, the plaintiff was irresponsible enough to seek the advice of a psychic. I rest my case!" There are psychics who can read minds. In forty years I've never met one.

I can't go around announcing that I 'read'. My IQ comes into question. People roll their eyes, there is a stigma still attached. Even open minded people are afraid that I know everybody's secrets. I've been blamed for bad weather, and even solar eclipses. I can only read in the quiet of my home with my rock on my solar plexus. Sure, many times, especially with meeting a new person, scenes pop into my mind, but I don't have time in a social setting to interpret what I am picking up and so it goes away.

The new fashion, readers operating from a psychic hotline, is for the most part ridiculous. I have been approached to become a part of that business and the money is great. But think about it – no reader can be good every day, every hour. They end up depending on the client giving them clues. Anybody could go with those and deliver a believable and, hopefully, an in-depth reading; the longer, the better, because the charges are by the minute. These hotline readers deliver a bunch of nonsense, vague references to riches just around the next corner. All of us love to hear that there is money ahead. Trips are another favorite. "I see you going on a long trip." Who doesn't at least go to a neighboring city; and the gullible then justify that prediction.

I can't justify those readings. People hear only what they want to hear. The psychic hotline is changing the world of psychics, just as our world has been changed by television and computers. Gone, mostly, is the one on one with a lighted candle and a bit of tingling mystery in the reader's clothing and their surroundings. I believe that something good has been lost. I like tea leaves, crystal balls, and a strange deck of tarot cards. Give me the black velvet and the incense.

Most of all, there is significant danger in relying on any information gained by way of a psychic for making any important decision. We, even the good and honest ones, have off days like everyone else. For example, suppose you want to leave your mate? You might be told that your mate is going to die soon. Is this coming from something in your subconscious? You decide to wait for any number of reasons. Nothing happens and you have changed the trajectory of your life based on faulty information. Buy or sell stock? Excuse me, not on your life!

Fortune telling has no place in one's life except as tongue-in-cheek entertainment. Go to a psychic in that spirit. Have fun. Don't build your hopes and dreams on their prophecy. They could have been coming down with a bad case of diarrhea.

If you want to have the experience of visiting a psychic, seek out one who has been recommended by friends, not always foolproof, but better than nothing. Don't offer any information. Give a 'yes' or 'no' answer to most questions. Do be encouraging with a smile and a "Yes!" I have always suspected questions; they are usually not legitimate. This technique is called "fishing" on the part of the reader. It seems wrong to go to a reading with mistrust, but that's my best advice.

It has been suggested that I should say something about intuition. I'm not sure how much intuition is included with true readings. All my readings come from another dimension and once I have "read" for a person, I cannot remember what I said to them. They have tapes; they can listen to them. I have nothing left from them but their money. When I have "read" for them, I usually cannot recall. If I had impressions of them, I usually cannot remember. So if it is partly intuition, I am not aware. I suppose I do have some intuition, but there again, do I?

Ralph Waldo Emerson wrote in his collection of essays entitled, "The Conduct of Life," *God builds his temple in the heart on the ruins of churches and religions.* Emerson wrote his version of that concept in 1860, how far back through the centuries was this first recognized, and yet we still have not understood this simple profound truth. God is in his temple, in our hearts, why have we ever looked elsewhere?

Religion Here and Now

Because The Bible and other sacred scriptures are considered to be unquestionable, the level of our religious understanding has remained equally unquestioned. So we have been left with views much more appropriate to the understanding of the dark ages than of the twenty-first century.

I believe my thoughts have created my reality. This is a law of our universe that takes some discipline and lots of practice. Every day, with every thought, we are creating our future. What do you want to accomplish, to have? Think of it daily. When a negative thought enters your mind, dismiss it immediately and replace it with thoughts of what you desire, especially illness! Refuse to be ill. Worry must be replaced with thoughts of perfect health. Claim health for yourself in the NOW, not worrying about how you, personally, can accomplish this miracle, but just let go and expect and accept perfect health. This is a philosophy based on love and acceptance of the God within, in contrast to the fear-based dictates of an outside authority. It replaces that judgmental God of our childhood. He does not imprison us with ultimatums, commandments, and fear of punishment. We do that ourselves. It has helped me to find my way back to the loving God I always dreamed of as being my God.

Do you desire a beautiful home? Treat the one you presently have with love. Forgive your house for not being the house you dreamed of having. Watch it turn into your perfect surroundings. Never criticize where you live. You created it with your thoughts. Does that knowledge sting? You can change it for the future and the same with the people around you. A favorite truth of mine, "If you love your enemies, you have no enemies." Command yourself to love SOMETHING about them and they will change into people you can enjoy or they will disappear from your life. Does it happen overnight? Sometimes. When you generate power to send something to someone – healing perhaps – it builds up in you first. It goes THROUGH you. So you get the benefit of it first, good or bad. Isn't that wonderful? You keep the original. They only receive the carbon copy.

If you do not have the virtue of patience, assume it; pretend that you are very patient and you will become patient. It is so simple, so very simple and most of us miss this wonderful truth.

The actor Cary Grant often said, "I pretended to be somebody I wanted to be until finally I became that person. Or he became me."

I learned to control anger with questioning myself each time I become angry with another person – did they attack my worth or my competency? EVERY TIME it is either one or the other and I could then laugh at myself and tell myself, once again, that I was of great worth, and great competency. I no longer worry about what others think of me. I know they seldom do!

Do you want the perfect mate? Write down exactly what you want down to the smallest of details, color of hair and eyes, etcetera. It took me two years of reading my list everyday but what's two years in a lifetime? I had even written down details of the sex life I desired. I thought of this person every day. He came from an unexpected direction. Sam was close to perfect. Of course, no man is perfect – oh, girls! Do not concern yourself with how it will happen. Importantly, think what your perfect mate would want for himself or herself. This might be painful, but should get you going on changing yourself for the better. And you are not responsible for change in anyone but yourself.

How? Seek ye first the Kingdom. Improve your spiritual life with books and various versions of audiobooks. A good place to start is with John Randolph Price's life changing book, *Superbeings*.

Then go on to read everything he's ever published. If you do not enjoy reading, you can find his works in audiobook format. His works, in many formats, are also available online along with many other metaphysical books.

Matthew 6:33, "But seek ye first the Kingdom of God, and his righteousness; and all these things shall be added unto you."

I consider this the most important advice in The Bible. This says it ALL. If you sincerely seek to become more spiritual – not religious – it is promised you that everything you need will be yours. Not what we think we need, but everything we really need before we even ask it or realize we need it. We must remember that the Kingdom of God is within us. Not somewhere up in the wild, blue yonder.

Understanding my intimate relationship with God as it is within me did not happen to me quickly. I would think, as I read, 'Yes, this is my truth,' but it took a while for the information to become a part of my everyday actions. Give yourself the gift of patience. Learn all you can about what our great minds have written down to help us. You are not a worm in the dust, doomed to an everlasting Hell. You have never done anything to be SAVED from. God is LOVE, pure love, sees only the good in us. He never doubts that you will just naturally, ultimately rejoin the all of Him and be at peace.

There are many ways to find peace in this life. There is no single method that everyone must follow. But I found my own peace by assuming I already had it – that ole 'fake it till you make it' and 'when the student is ready, the teacher will appear' was what I practiced. Books FELL into my lap, given to me by friends, checked out at the library for their interesting titles, cover art, etcetera. It worked. I am always at peace now.

As soon as I began studying spiritually my finances improved. Things I needed came to me from many directions as if by magic. People who once gave me problems either moved away or drifted away. I found new friends who were also on the path of seeking the kingdom. We are all drawn to each other, renewing ancient connections.

If you are in an abusive relationship, get out of it. Spirituality cannot flower where cruelty lives. Don't allow anyone to tell you that you cannot make it on your own, are too dumb to support yourself, are too homely – the list with a verbally abusive partner goes on and on. Dare to be free. You won't starve. Life is difficult enough without wasting your energy on a losing battle by subjugating your own personality. I'd clean houses if nothing else were available.

I learned two very valuable things from Maya Perez. First, when paying with cash, fold paper money in half and with both ends pointing to you, hand them the money, with the folded side to the receiver. This tells your money to return to you double. It has worked! I have never been broke since I trained myself to always present money with the ends coming back to me. Second, I write checks in this fashion, xxx/xxxx, in the cents column. It means, "I love you" (xxx) and "Thank you, infinite supply" (xxxx). For thirty years, I've never been overdrawn. I also keep a two-dollar bill (banks have them) in my wallet, folded up very small. It is seed-money. Money attracts money. NEVER spend it, not for any emergency. Thank you, Maya.

The greatest thing to come out of my freeing myself was meeting my new husband. He is gone now after nineteen wonderful years.

While I was driving alone to Dallas to visit my daughter and he was at home, the following poem came to me. It underlines how perfect our time together was for me. I had to set it to paper before it escaped me. I was driving sixty mph with no time to stop. I reached behind me to the back seat where my notebook always rides, with no real hope that I could reach it. I pulled that yellow pad right out, wrote down this poem with keeping my eyes on the road. I've always scolded my son for his habit of driving and reading. Sorry about that son, sometimes it is necessary.

The day before this poem came to me I'd finished Jess Stern's book *SoulMates*. He was a friend of my friend, Maya. Now after four years of its hiding after I wrote it, I uncovered my poem. My love, Sam, has made his transition so it is nice for me to have my poem as a reminder.

On Jess Stern's *SoulMates*

I, too, the common misconception bought
Of soul mate's rare appearance, clarion call
And trumpets blazing, lights lit up
Brass bands and fireworks and stars.
In former love connections, suffered all
Fights, fists, yells, tantrums, tears.
Lonely times and sky-high thrills, rejections,
And start again once more.
Almost unnoticed, then he came along.
A quiet man, programmed by me and long lost hope.
Strong man, well loved by family for his truth,
Words spoken never doubted, always fair.
A handsome man, broad-shouldered, flat of girth.
Laughter rumbling just beneath a surface calm
And such a love of far placed lands
And curious, too, to know the where and what
Of all this earth.
But best and most of all – we fit just right
On politics and love and larger matters, too,
The easy warmth, the camaraderie
The comfort of acceptance.
A day-by-day existence easy now
The wonder of it all I cannot quite believe
Mate of my soul, here, home with me!
                              -to Sam with love, June

I did my last professional reading on a dark and bitter, cold and rainy night in 1982. It was winter and the rain had turned to sleet. The Dallas Police Department called me to ask for my help in finding a small girl who had been abducted two days earlier. They want to try anything in times where they possibly have no clues to work from so it's, 'Lord, I believe. Help Thou my unbelief,' time about psychics. There's no publicity or even much credit from the department, but thank goodness the police do recognize we often can be of help. I told them that I would try my best.

I lit a candle, put my geode on my tummy and turned on the tape recorder, opening myself to any information. Then, soon, in my mind, I was outside in the sleet and sensing the bitter cold. There was a road under me that I felt was out of the city and a ditch running alongside. I hovered over the ditch seeing a small body. It was a female child. She was alive! Her only clothing was a short undershirt. From her waist down her small form was nude. She was almost covered with leaves but it was not a protection from the sleeting rain. I was frantic. Where were we? Where was this road, this ditch? I looked in all directions for any sign of any kind, a farmhouse, a barn, a town, a signpost, anything to give the police as a geographic marker.

I felt myself spinning. Being out of my body this time was a horrible experience. I'd never felt so frantic. When I panicked, I was immediately back in my body. The reunion was an uncomfortable bump. I lay there, back in my bed, trying to return to the ditch. Nothing I tried helped me overcome my panic. This child was dying. Why had I been shown that pitiful scene and not have been given more information? The tape I'd been making ended in my cries and was of no use but they came and collected it anyway. I was ashamed of finding the abducted girl without being of any more help.

All that night I tried to find her again! I never slept. I alternately sweated and went into chills. I vomited twice. There was no peace for me. I knew time was running out. The sleet hitting my roof went through me like dozens of knife-points cutting me to pieces. Nothing!

What had my psychic life been about, just entertainment for bored housewives, 'desperate housewives'? My ability is called a "Gift." There was no gift in what I was going through – only Hell. I knew our 'days were numbered' but that old saw didn't help. I was accustomed to getting just bits and pieces, sure, but tonight was different. In reading, clients had accepted this problem and seemed contented with what I could divine. They waited to see what would happen. Well, this time there was no time to wait. I prayed and cried to God for help, knowing that was not how one accomplishes anything. Prayer is not telling God what to do. Prayer is not to change God's attitude. Real prayer is to be sensitive and receptive. I failed. I then mentally put blankets around the child. I held the vision of her to my breast to warm her.

Two days later they found her in a ditch, covered in leaves, wearing only an undershirt. She was dead.

I was finished with reading for people who wanted a thrill, wanted predictions of excitements to come. I told customers I was taking a needed sabbatical. I have never done another professional reading. Reluctantly, I read for the family, but I now have lost interest in the whole process. I admire seers who can be of help. There are many, many good ones. I met a good one, a man in Houston, Texas who reads from photographs. The minute he met me he was alarmed. He told me I was a reader who was not doing readings and warned me that if I did not use my talent I would die. That was twelve years ago. I'm still hangin' out. I've denied his prediction even though I thought he was excellent. I feel I have many more years left. Who knows, I may write another book someday.

Love and light to you. Bless you on your way.

ABOUT THE AUTHOR

This book, *Secrets of a Psychic,* is the story of June Campobello's adventure in self-discovery and exploration of the mysteries within her that created the magnificent person she has become. This short biography, *About the Author*, has been lovingly put together by members of her family. At issue for us was what would June choose for her "author name" and thought she might have wanted to use a "nom de plume."

During her early experiences as a young psychic, she had a different first and last name. As the wife and ex-wife of her first husband, she used her middle name and her first husband's name. Neither seem to fit the person she is today. Finally, she combined her middle name, June, with her soul mate/second husband's last name, Campobello, and that is the name she has chosen to use as an author. Over these last twenty years living in the Texas hill country and in her beloved Dallas, she has become that unique "Auntie Mame-ish" writer and artist, June Campobello, who never disappoints!

June recently celebrated her birthday with about fifty family members and friends at her favorite Mexican restaurant in Plano, Texas. She happily unveiled the proof of her book and her plans for publication. Her fans were delighted.

The publication of this book is a tribute to the tenacity and exuberance June has always demonstrated for life. Her characteristic passion for love and to be loved, to have great fun with respect for others, to cherish life, to jealously guard her right to enjoy art, literature, music, travel, family, friends and relationships have been the model for teaching all of us the art of living.

As you read this book, you begin to understand what June has had to learn and overcome in order to be true to herself. Each phase of her life was important to that development. She is of Scandinavian heritage and lived in the mid-west in her early life. Her family then moved to Texas, where she has lived at various times in the Tyler, San Antonio, and Dallas areas. Being accepted as a psychic or supported as an artist has not always been easy.

Her first marriage to Jack Coulter, a handsome and charming Texan who served in World War II, produced two extraordinary children; Alan, who is a respected psychologist living in the New Orleans area, and Trish, a beautiful, accomplished woman now working in real estate finance in Plano. June and Jack divorced in 1967. After several years, they worked out a friendly divorce relationship in behalf of their children in great part due to June's understanding of Karmic relationships.

While working as a celebrated business person in Dallas (often top salesperson for her company), June had the chance to fulfill her lifelong love of travel to foreign exotic places. Among those places, she traveled to Egypt and amazed the grandchildren with a picture of Mama June riding a camel near one of the Great Pyramids.

June married Sam Campobello, a handsome Italian widower in 1982, who had been a part of her earlier social circle. Sam was a World War II Veteran. He was a Certified Public Accountant by vocation, and an glass-artist/woodworker by avocation. Living in the Hill Country, all of their artistic talents flourished. One of their joint projects was completion of a series of 26 stained-glass windows depicting the stories from The Bible. They were designed by June for the New Braunfels' Lutheran Church, and were completed and installed in the church by Sam and June. The church also produced a booklet featuring the windows with accompanying script and pictures in black and white, so children could color in the stain-glass windows as they learned the stories.

While living in the Hill Country, the couple became members of the Quartus Foundation, founded in part and nurtured by the authors, John and Jan Price. The Price's and the Campobello's enjoyed a wonderful relationship of many, many years, along with other members of Quartus. Sam Campobello and Jan Price are both gone now, but as you might imagine, they both remain with us in spirit.

June and Sam lived happily for many years in their geodesic dome house in the Hill Country, built by Sam and decorated by June using stained-glass designs for emphasis. What parties! What holidays! We will never forget!

Once married to Sam, travel became a major part of their lives. June got to see her Scandinavian homeland, the Campobello family's Italian birthplace, other European sites, and New Zealand where they had always wanted to go. She has enjoyed Manhattan (in New York City) and the wonderful museums, but still has Paris on the list for where to go next. All of these experiences have been a part of and tied to her art, her writing, and has helped shape her exuberant personality.

June has always been on an artistic and literary journey throughout her life, marked early in her career by an art scholarship, and reinforced by the understanding that she could, through reading, museum study, and learning from colleagues, be a part of the world that would refine the talents that she had been given. She has passed this understanding onto her children. June has always practiced her art and enjoys the company and collegiality of other artists to this day. She is now giving art lessons to friends who come to her home to learn from her, and says she always learns equally from them.

June's health has always been exceptional and she has been able to overcome health problems that might have taken down a lesser individual. June has recovered completely from a cerebellar brain bleed several years ago. However, no longer being able to drive really "pisses" her off. We think she finally accepts the wisdom of that one limitation!

June's extended family now includes: two children and five grandchildren and their respective spouses, 10 great-grandchildren and their spouses, and 3 great-great grandchildren. She refuses to call them greats; the are all grands! She is known to us as Grand MaMa or MaMa June, depending if she is in Texas, Georgia, Louisiana, North Carolina, or at the beach on the Gulf Coast of Alabama. The gift she gives to all of us is unconditional love, and we are thankful. Everyone should have a MaMa June in their life. It is very difficult to get a good count (as the list keeps growing) of her friends, colleagues, and the caring personnel who keep her going every day. They all marvel at her spunk and her tenacity. If you have an opportunity to meet June Campobello, take it! You won't be sorry.

Made in the USA
Charleston, SC
26 July 2013